D1539093

Completing Life

By

Rabbi Sidney Greenberg

© 2004 by Rabbi Sidney Greenberg. All rights reserved.

No part of this book may be reproduced, stored in a retrieval system, or transmitted by any means, electronic, mechanical, photocopying, recording, or otherwise, without written permission from the author.

ISBN: 1-4107-2971-0 (e-book)
ISBN: 1-4107-2972-9 (Paperback)

This book is printed on acid free paper.

1stBooks – rev. 04/12/04

ACKNOWLEDGEMENTS

When my husband departed from this world swiftly and without warning, he had not yet completed the editing of the manuscript for this book. I could not possibly have accomplished this monumental task without the invaluable assistance of a loyal, generous, and dedicated group of individuals. I would therefore like to express my gratitude to the following people for helping me to carry out this labor of love:

Robert Kanter, our dear friend, and Rabbi Jay Stein, our esteemed colleague, for their thoughtful review of the sermons;

Karen Wilder, our diligent and faithful typist, for her intensive labor and attention to myriad details;

Pamela Zimmerman, our skilled editor, for her unusual talent, efficiency, and creativity;

Asya Berger, our dear friend, for her generosity of spirit and for the expert proficiency with which she accomplished the final proofreading of this manuscript; and

Dr. Adena Greenberg, our beloved daughter, for the countless hours she invested in ensuring that this book would remain true to the high standards of excellence that her father embraced in his life and work.

Hilda Greenberg

Dedication

Dedicated with love to the memory of my very dear friends
Ruth and Budd Rockower
and their daughter, Carol Goldstein,
and with gratitude to their children, grandchildren, and great
grandchildren
whose generosity made the publication of this book possible.

Mark John Goldstein
David Manuel Goldstein
Robert Rockower Goldstein
Thomas Zoltan Greenwald
Lynda Joy Greenwald
Tyler Clayton Greenwald
Brayden Goldstein Greenwald
Spencer Leyland Greenwald
Joan Rockower Greenfield
William S. Greenfield
Lauren Greenfield
Gregory Treat Lanham
Alexis Greenfield Lanham
Andrew Treat Lanham
Jill Greenfield Feldman
Ronald P. Feldman
Rachel Michelle Feldman
Debra Beth Feldman
Amy Lynne Feldman
Michael William Greenfield
Benjamin Rockower Greenfield
Elayn (Elana) Rockower Ponet
James Ponet
David Lev Ponet
Daniella Ponet
Avital Ponet
Shulamit Rachel Ponet

CONTENTS

FOREWORD

In "A Word to the Reader," from *Adding Life to Our Years* (1959), his second book but first sermon collection, my father, Sidney Greenberg, wrote:

> In the sixteen years I have been preaching, I have never approached the preparation of a sermon or its delivery without a potent dose of what our sages called, *"emata d'tziburah* – awe of the congregation." This quaking sense of apprehension is fearfully intensified as these sermons are released for publication.

This phrase, *emata d'tziburah*, captured my attention as I contemplated writing this foreword to the posthumous publication of my father's fourth collection of sermons and thirty-third book. On the morning of his sudden death, my father was working on this volume, hoping to complete it that day. Instead, his life unexpectedly ended and we, his loved ones, were left with the privilege and daunting task of completing his final sermon collection, prophetically titled, *Completing Life.* While my own sense of *emata d'tziburah* derives somewhat from what my father once called "the awesome finality of the printed page," it stems more from the inner imperative to adequately and fully honor his memory and pay tribute to his vast and rich legacy.

Having taught homiletics at rabbinical seminaries and lectured at sermon seminars around the country, my father has been widely recognized as a master of homiletics – the art of preaching. With utmost dedication to informing and inspiring through sermons, he wholeheartedly devoted himself to what he referred to as "the onerous task and fierce discipline of sermon preparation." Indeed, the publisher of his High Holiday sermon collection, *Hidden Hungers* (1972), wrote on the jacket cover:

> Each sermon is carefully thought out, finely structured, and vividly illustrated in a way that is compelling and

ix

unforgettable. The style is beautiful and direct; the message clear and compelling.

My father's mind was a treasure trove of words and stories, quotes and quips. These he wove together, with skill and artistry, to poetically deliver powerful messages of Jewish content, social relevance, and personal meaning. His material is enriched by his vast knowledge of Jewish text, tradition, liturgy, and history as well as of world literature, culture, history, and events. His writings are indeed a masterful integration of Jewish and secular, ancient and modern, universal and personal, spiritual and practical.

My father's gifts of mind and intellect were richly enhanced by his gifts of spirit and soul. Thus, the wisdom in his many volumes is further imbued with the gentle sensitivity of his soul, the humility of his spirit, the warmth, humor, and charm of his personality, and the unconditional quality of his love for God and humanity.

My mother, his beloved companion for more than 60 years, has frequently reflected aloud that she and my father carefully discussed and planned for the many issues that would arise at the time of their inevitable separation from each other in this world. Yet, they had never spoken about how his unpublished manuscripts would be handled in the event that his death preceded their publication. As I saw it, my father probably never worried about the future of these writings because he instinctively counted on my mother to anticipate and fulfill his every need – even in death. Without having to think about it, he knew that she would take care of his unfinished business, when death came to call, just as she had conscientiously and lovingly tended to his needs during their many years together.

In "A Word to the Reader," [from *Adding Life to Our Years* (1959)], my father paid specific tribute to my mother's significant role in the creation of his sermons:

My beloved wife and helpmate, Hilda, is part of these sermons in a most vital way. She attended their birth and agonized through their delivery. Her availability at all times as an audience of one contributed immeasurably to the refinement of the ideas in their developmental stages. The congregation, the reader,

x

and I are also deeply indebted to her for many a sermon I did not preach.

And so, in my father's death as in his life, my mother has faithfully devoted herself to all that was sacred to him. With the publication of this book, she carries forward the abiding values and spirit of his life and his life's work with passion and dedication. And we, the readers, are enormously fortunate that she has done so, confident in the knowledge that these writings will enrich our learning, challenge our thinking, and uplift our spirits. From "day one" of what would become his 54 years of congregational service, my father's mission naturally became their shared mission. Theirs was a rare and enduring partnership of devotion to each other, to family, to their congregation, and to everything that Judaism holds sacred. The spirit of their blessed union will endure long beyond their physical separation from each other.

To address the content of this precious volume, I would like to focus on the title my father chose: *Completing Life*. What does it mean to "complete life?" Several weeks before his untimely death, my father was close to finishing several manuscripts and was asked, "So what are you going to write about next?" The question was prompted by the fact that he was always working on a book. Quite surprisingly, he answered, "I think I'm finished. I've said all I wanted to say." What an extraordinary notion! To approach the end of life with the sense of having completed one's intended goals – to close one's eyes at the end of life's journey, content in the knowledge that one has fulfilled one's ultimate purpose and promise in this life! How does one reach this enviable point in life – and in my father's case, point of departure *from* life – as one moves closer and closer to the end?

I believe that the wisdom my father has bequeathed to us in these writings will help us wrestle with this enormous challenge. Taken individually and collectively, his sermons guide, encourage, and inspire us in our struggle to find meaning and purpose in our lives – in our striving to not simply *end* life but to *complete* life, inwardly gratified by having realized our own potentials and goals.

Just perusing the tables of contents of my father's books, one sees that each sermon or essay is intended to assist us in "adding life to our years" in making our lives and ourselves more "complete." As suggested by two of his other book titles, his sermons assist us with addressing our *Hidden Hungers* and *Finding Ourselves.* In his life and work, my father grappled unceasingly with every facet of the human condition. His ultimate and overriding desire was to endlessly encourage, inspire, and exhort us to make the most of ourselves and to help us meet the challenges we would inevitably confront in our encounters with others, with God, and with ourselves.

My father understood how inextricably linked and interdependent we human beings are. As he reminds us in his sermon titled, "We All Lean," we rely on each other for favors, large and small, and we bring meaning to our own lives when we give to others. We have moral obligations to one another. He suggests that we use the values of Judaism and the Torah to guide our thinking and fortify our moral integrity when we find ourselves in "The Valley of Decision." He counsels us to "repair relationships" by examining our angers, resentments, and prejudices.

In "Lessons in a Hospital Bed," my father describes his own "mindfulness of blessings" and abundant "gratitude in the face of adversity." In "Losses," he recognizes the inevitability of loss of all kinds but also the gains that can accompany it. There he tells us that it is only through loss that we can become fully developed human beings. No one is spared loss, disappointment, anguish, or suffering – a subject that he explored in a sermon titled "Covering Our Sackcloths." Challenged with the greatest loss of all, that of his first-born child (my sister, Shira), he himself struggled with "Finding God in Great Loss."

Grappling with evils beyond our control, my father's faith in God prompted him to enjoin *us* to have faith. Even when writing during the darkest chapter in recent Jewish history, the Nazis' extermination of the six million, my father urged us to maintain hope in the face of despair, courage and determination in the face of suffering.

In this connection, I am cognizant of an unusual and valuable dimension of these writings: spanning six decades of American and Jewish life, they offer fascinating perspectives on major cultural, political, and historical events of the day. The collection represents one rabbi's attempts to wrestle – on behalf of his congregation, his people, his family, and indeed of all humanity – with anti-Semitism, political corruption, and racial injustice. Yet at the same time, he also celebrates the creation of the State of Israel, the stunning achievements of that tiny country, and the flowering of Conservative Judaism.

Irrespective of external events, however, my father implored us to never stop developing ourselves internally. For "in our heart of hearts, we each know that we were meant to keep growing as long as we keep breathing." Indeed, in every area of life, we are "always capable of improving." This we should do not only for our own sake but also for the sake of others, present and future, whose lives we influence. There is:

> …no ceiling on our attainment…no limit on what we can become…. We each have boundless resources of mind and spirit waiting to be tapped, imprisoned splendor waiting to be released, vast potential waiting to become real.

And so, in keeping with my father's wise counsel, it is incumbent upon us, in our hour of grief, to turn our sorrow and longing into an opportunity for growth. Just as my father completed his own life, so he helps us, through the legacy of his life and writings, to complete our own. Finally, if we "complete as much of our lives as possible before they are finished," we will also help each other to grow into the better and larger selves that he fervently believed we each could become.

Adena Greenberg
September 2003 / Elul 5763
New York, New York

INSPIRATION

Don't Stop Growing

Be it ever so humble, there's no verse in the Torah from which a vital lesson cannot be distilled. Consider, for example, this prosaic-looking phrase in this week's Torah portion: "When an ox or a sheep, or a goat is born…" (*Leviticus* 22:27).

All right, we say, so what's so special about these words? What have we to do with an ox or a sheep or a goat? Only this, according to one Jewish interpreter of our Torah:

> An ox at birth is called an ox. A goat is called a goat at birth. They have each reached their maximum potential at the very beginning. A four-year-old ox is not kinder, more understanding or more helpful than a four-day-old goat.

Quite otherwise is the situation with humans. At birth we are not called adults. We come into the world as infants who must go through various stages of growth before we become adults. We're not born human. At birth, we are candidates for humanity.

And this growth is not merely a physical process. It is not automatic. It involves profound dimensions of mind, spirit, and personality. The human being must want to grow and be ready to contribute to this growth and development through great personal striving and sustained, dedicated effort.

A third-grader taught his teacher this important truth: "How many great men," she asked, "were born in our city?"

"None," replied the pupil. "There were no great men born. They were born babies who became great men."

Greatness may not be within the reach of every one of us but growth is. We are each capable of being a more mature person today than we were yesterday, and tomorrow can find us further along than we are today. And when we forget this vital truth, we have lost sight of the essential meaning of life and the source of its deepest fulfillment.

Successful living is measured not in terms of what we acquire but in what we become. It comes not from outside us, but from within. Because so many of us miss this point, my friend, Rabbi

Harold Kushner, wrote a book entitled, *When All You've Ever Wanted Isn't Enough.* Why isn't it enough when we acquire all the material things we thought would bring us happiness?

The answer is to be found in the nature of our beings. We need the material things to enable us to survive with more or less comfort. But essentially we are spiritual beings and it is there that we must look for fulfillment.

Among his literary remains, Nathaniel Hawthorne left notebooks which contain random ideas he jotted down as they occurred to him. One of the short entries reads, "Suggestions for a story in which the principal character never appears."

Unhappily, this is the story of too many lives. The principal character simply never appears. The person we might grow into, the human being we might become, doesn't show up.

When we stop growing morally, spiritually, and intellectually, we find a sense of discontent gnawing at us. We become "sick with unused self," to use the phrase of an astute observer of the human condition. We remain haunted by the "principal character" that invades our dreams at night and mars our serenity by day. In our heart of hearts, we each know that we were meant to keep growing as long as we keep breathing.

If a seed in its dark, restless journey underground is not content until it breaks through the mountain of soil and strains ever higher toward the sunlight, shall we human beings be content to remain like an ox or a goat at the point where it all began?

When he was 90 years old, Pablo Casals, the renowned cellist, was asked: "Why do you still practice so many hours a day?" He answered simply, "Because I think I am improving."

In every significant area of life, we are constantly capable of improving. We can become more capable of forgiveness, more sensitive to another's pain, more receptive to criticism, more open to a new idea.

After teaching the biblical account of creation, the teacher asked one youngster, "Who made you?" The pupil gave this unexpected reply: "Well, to tell you the truth, I ain't made yet."

And neither is any one of us. Our principal character is still waiting to appear. Let's not keep him or her waiting too long.

1985/5745

3

Are There Any Corrections to the Minutes?

Thomas Mann has written: "Time has no division to mark its passage; there is never a thunderstorm or blare of trumpets to announce the beginning of a new month or year. Even when a new century begins, it is only we mortals who ring the bells and fire off the pistols!"

Mann was eminently correct. The moments tiptoe quietly by. It is we who build the watches and clocks to beat out the steady rhythm of their silent procession. Or perhaps time itself doesn't move at all as Austin Dobson has suggested in the poem, "The Paradox of Time":

"Time goes, you say? Ah, no! Alas, Time stays, we go."

But whether time is passing us or we are passing time, the beginning of a New Year on the civil calendar brings with it a host of different emotions depending upon our age, our achievements, or failures during the fading year, or our anticipations or fears for the year about to dawn. We face the New Year in a mood of suspense and mystery. Time has been correctly compared to:

A flower unblown,
A book unread,
A tree with fruit unharvested,
A path untrod,
A house whose rooms lack yet the heart's divine perfumes.

And it is this very quality of the New Year, its manifold possibilities, its unpredictable character, its very sure surprises, that provides the salty flavor of life. Tonight I should like to think with you not so much about what the New Year may bring to us, but rather about what we should and should not bring to the New Year. Let us consider first and primarily what we should not bring to the New Year.

One of the first orders of business at any organizational meeting is the reading of the minutes of the previous meeting. After the secretary has duly performed this routine task, the chairman will ask in equally routine fashion: "Are there any corrections to the minutes?" Then one member of the group, gifted with a long memory, will rise and say: "The minutes report that we allotted $12.95 for the auction publicity. The actual figure was $13.95."

Another type of correction may be offered by a second member: "The vehement disagreement between Arthur Cohen and George Lewin did take place but I move that it be stricken from the minutes. It will not make pretty reading to anyone going over our minutes. It will not enhance our prestige as a body." Most of the time this suggestion will prevail because, in retrospect, we realize that there are some things we do not wish to carry forward as part of the permanent record, even though they did in fact occur.

In similar fashion, I think that you and I ought to review our own minutes of the past year for the purpose of striking from them any entries which, in our more reflective moments, we should not want to carry forward into the New Year.

In the first place, I think we ought to try to strike from the minutes our accumulated resentments and angers. Too many of our angers are like inverted pyramids. They often rest on tiny, trivial incidents but they spread upward and outward until they fill our minds. In permitting them to do so, we render ourselves a lamentable disservice.

Anger, we should remember, is only one letter short of danger. Anger is a trait we share with the beasts. But the beast has this advantage over us. After the rage has been spent, the beast gives it no further thought, while man on the other hand will continue to fume and fret and fuss, nurse the anger along and continue to burn himself up with its flames long after the real or imagined provocation has vanished.

It is terribly expensive to perpetuate our resentments and bitterness. They occupy vital space that could more cheerfully and more soothingly be filled with beauty and loveliness. Resentment, medical studies indicate, is a frequent cause of headaches, indigestion, fatigue, insomnia, and high blood pressure. Angry people have increased proneness to accidents. We pay exorbitantly for hurts we cherish and the wounds we keep open.

In the 16th chapter of the *Book of Proverbs*, we read that "He that is slow to anger is better than the mighty, and he that ruleth his spirit than he that taketh a city." Admittedly, being "slow to anger" is

5

a most admirable trait. Those of us who are fortunate to possess what psychologists call "a high threshold," those who are not easily upset or distressed, are to be much envied. But even if we are quick to anger, short of temper, and lacking in patience, we can yet strive to "rule our spirits." After we have indulged our anger, blown off our fury, we ought not nourish endlessly the bitter grapes of wrath.

I respectfully move, my friends, that we strike from the minutes of our lives our accumulated resentments and angers if we are to conduct the business of living efficiently and happily in 1957.

A second item most deserving of obliteration from the minutes of our lives is prejudice. Prejudice has been defined as "being positive about something negative." Originally prejudice was a neutral word, meaning simply, to prejudge, to form a judgment beforehand without sufficient evidence. It might be a favorable judgment or an unfavorable one. But so prone are we to form negative judgments without adequate justification that the term, "prejudice" came to mean exclusively injurious judgment.

We, of all people, ought to be most sensitive to the insidious evil inherent in prejudice. Prejudice, like a haunting shadow, has stalked the Jew throughout his painful pilgrimage and has exacted a staggering toll of innocent victims.

It is, therefore, doubly distressing to see this evil take root in Jewish minds. Too often bigoted statements against members of other minority groups are heard in our midst. We are too prone to accept uncritically the cheap currency of the marketplace as reflective of the true worth of others. And often, in our estimate of one another, we are inclined to form injurious judgments without sufficient justification.

Why do we, who should know better, succumb to the all-too-human temptation to adopt prejudices? The answer, I suppose, is to be found in the fact that prejudice is useful in many ways.

In the first place, it is a great time-saver. It enables us to form opinions without bothering to get the facts. Once having made up our minds, there is no need to trouble ourselves to re-examine our views. "A great many people," wrote William James, "think they are thinking when they are merely rearranging their prejudices." We become like the old theologian who declared that he was entirely open to conviction but he defied anybody to convince him.

Prejudice also helps us to project our faults onto others. Our sages cautioned on one occasion: "The fault that resides within you, do not attribute to your neighbor." Again they warned: "He who declares another unfit does so with his own blemish." Our wise men recognized the ruse our mind plays on us by getting us to dislike in others those faults of ours which our self-love prevents us from unmasking in ourselves.

A third function prejudice performs for us is to inflate our starved egos. The smarter we are, the stronger the urge to cut someone else down to the point where we can look down upon him. Prejudice is a psychological stilt that makes us appear taller than we are. Who will deny that we can conduct the business of living in 1957 more humanely if we strike from our minutes our accumulated prejudices?

Lastly, may I suggest that we strike from the minutes of the past all our futile regrets? All of us have heard or quoted Whittier's well-known lines, "Of all sad words of tongue or pen, the saddest are these, 'It might have been.'" Bret Harte amplified this by saying, "If, of all sad words of tongue or pen, the saddest are, 'It might have been,' more sad are these we daily see, 'It is, but it hadn't ought to be.'"

While we're at it, we might recall what Guy Wetmore Carryl did with Whittier's lines in a poem entitled, "How Jack Found That Beans May Go Back on a Chap." The moral is that gardeners pine whenever no pods adorn the vine. "Of all sad words experience gleans, the saddest are 'It might have beens.'" (I did not make this up myself. 'Twas in a book upon my shelf. It is witty, but I don't deny it's rather Whittier than I.)

Yes, all the "might have beens" and "it hadn't ought to be's"– the wonderful things that might have been and aren't, the melancholy events that hadn't ought to be and are – is any life free from them? Is there any record in which they did not make their sad entries in 1956? Unfulfilled hopes, blasted dreams, interrupted melodies – who does not know of them? Yet, must we perpetuate these? Must we continue to pay compound interest upon losses incurred and profits unattained? We do precisely that when we permit our vain regrets to extort their merciless toll, to blackmail our promising todays by dangling before us the harrowing skeleton of our bleak yesterdays.

7

A mother explained the word "budget" to her inquiring daughter by saying that "A budget is a method of worrying before you spend instead of afterward." Vain regret might then be defined as paying for something both when you buy it and forever afterward. Life is difficult enough. Why do we have to add to our burdens by encumbering ourselves with all our accumulated failures and disappointments? It is not our defeats, losses, and mistakes we ought to perpetuate but whatever lessons and insights we were wise enough to distill from them. How wise we would be to follow the wholesome advice of Omar Khayyam: "Ah, my dear, drain the cup that clears today of past regrets and future fears."

May I move, dear friends, that we do just that – that we strike from the minutes of our lives all encumbering and futile regrets?

By way of concluding our thought, I'd like to change our metaphor from the minutes of a meeting to a recipe for the New Year, which I chanced upon recently and which I'd like to leave with you in slightly modified form. The recipe sums up our own thoughts concerning the ingredients we ought to leave out, and goes on to tell us what ingredients we ought to include, to make 1957 the rewarding adventure it can be:

RECIPE FOR A HAPPY NEW YEAR

"Take twelve fine, full-grown months. See that these are thoroughly free from old memories of bitterness, rancor, hate, and jealousy. Cleanse them completely from every clinging regret; pick off all specks of pettiness and prejudice. In short, see that these months are freed from all past gripes and grievances. Have them as fresh and clean as when they first came from the great storehouse of time.

Cut these months into 30 or 31 equal parts. This batch will keep for just one year. Do not attempt to make up the whole batch at one time (so many people spoil the entire lot this way), but prepare one day at a time as follows:

Into each day put 12 parts of faith, 11 of patience, 10 of courage, 9 of work (some people omit this ingredient and spoil the flavor of the rest), 8 parts of hope, 7 of fidelity, 6 of liberality, 5 of kindness, 4 of rest (leaving this out is like leaving the oil out of the salad – don't do it), 3 parts of prayer, 2 of meditation, and 1 well-selected resolution.

Then put in about a teaspoonful of good spirits, a dash of fun, a pinch of folly, a jigger of laughter, a sprinkling of play, and a heaping cup of good humor.

Cook thoroughly in a fervent heat.

Garnish with a few smiles and a sprig of joy.

Then serve with quietness, unselfishness, and cheerfulness and a Happy Year is a certainty."

1957/5717

Forget About Excuses

Choosing a wife for oneself is an awesome responsibility; choosing a wife for someone else is infinitely more so. But this is precisely the mission that Abraham assigns to his wise and faithful steward when he sends Eliezer to select a wife for his son, Isaac.

What criterion should Eliezer use for his choice? Abraham does not tell him. Apparently, he trusts Eliezer's judgment – in this matter, more than he trusts his own.

Having arrived at his destination, Eliezer waits at the well at the outskirts of the city, where the women come at evening to draw water. Then he offers this prayer:

> O Lord, God of my master Abraham, grant me good fortune this day, and deal graciously with my master Abraham: Here I stand by the spring as the daughters of the townsmen come out to draw water; let the maiden to whom I say, "Please, lower your jar that I may drink," and who replies, "Drink, and I will also water your camels," let her be the one whom You have decreed for Your servant Isaac. Thereby shall I know that You have dealt graciously with my master. (*Genesis* 24: 12-14)

Scarcely does he finish his prayer when Rebecca appears. To his request for water for himself, she graciously obliges and then, unsolicited, offers water for his camels, too. Eliezer is convinced that Rebecca is indeed worthy to become Isaac's wife and that his mission has been blessed with success.

The young lady's pre-eminent qualification was her willingness to give *more* than was asked of her. But as we reflect on the incident, we realize there were two additional considerations that convinced Eliezer that she indeed was destined (*bashert*) to become Abraham's daughter-in-law.

It was not only her willingness to give *more*, it was her willingness to give *at all*. She did have a perfect excuse for not acceding to Eliezer's request. She might have said, "You seem to be in good health, Mister. I see nothing wrong with you. Here's the pitcher; help yourself."

She had a very legitimate excuse – and did not use it.

I admire that quality in her. The glory of a human being lies in the ability to resist the temptation to offer an excuse rather than to offer help – to have a good excuse for not doing a kindness and not use the excuse.

On the day after I officiated at the wedding of a young lady, I called her hospitalized grandmother to cheer her up after what I knew must have been a great disappointment over missing her first grandchild's wedding. To my surprised delight, I heard a radiant voice at the other end of the phone, scarcely able to contain excitement.

"Rabbi," she bubbled, "You'll never guess what my Annie did yesterday morning. Before going to Temple Sinai to be married, she came here to me in my hospital room all dressed up in her wedding gown. If I live to be 120, I'll never forget her kindness."

Annie had a wonderful excuse for not visiting her grandmother in her wedding gown in the hours immediately preceding her wedding – and she did not use the excuse.

As we study the lives of great people, we come repeatedly upon this quality – the strength not to use a good excuse.

Milton had a great excuse for not writing deathless poetry. He was blind. Beethoven had a marvelous excuse for not composing immortal music. He was deaf. Louis Pasteur had a very persuasive excuse for not persisting in his scientific quest. He was paralyzed. Robert Louis Stevenson had a most compelling reason for not creating the literary classics we never outgrow. He was a life-long invalid, victimized by tuberculosis.

In grand achievement as in noble character, the secret is so often found in the courage not to use a good excuse.

Moreover, Rebecca impressed Eliezer not only by what she did, but also by *how* she did it.

Listen to the Torah's narrative:

And she said, "Drink my Lord" and she hastened and let down her pitcher and gave him drink. And when she had finished, she said, "I will draw water for your camel also." And she hastened and emptied her pitcher into the trough and *ran* again to the well. (*Genesis* 18:20)

Notice how eagerly she performs the *mitzvah* of kindness to strangers. She doesn't drag her feet. She shows no lingering reluctance. She "hastens," she "runs." Joyfully, zestfully, spontaneously, she responds to human need, obviously grateful for the privilege.

In this noble virtue, she emulated her soon-to-be father-in-law, Abraham, who *ran* toward approaching strangers, virtually pleading with them to accept his hospitality.

We give twice when we give quickly.

If you were Eliezer, would you have chosen Rebecca?

1992/5752

Take My Hand

Marcus Aurelius, the Roman philosopher, left us a great deal of wisdom in his *Meditations*, but I believe he was very wide of the mark when he wrote, "He is poor who stands in need of another and has not within himself all things needful for this life."

I wonder: is there anyone, anywhere, at any time who does not stand in need of another? Who indeed can imagine even for a moment that he has "within himself all things needful for this life?" Who does not realize how desperately dependent we are upon each other?

One of humanity's greatest benefactors, Albert Einstein, captured a profound truth when he wrote, "A hundred times a day I remind myself that my inner and outer life depends on the labors of other men, living and dead, and that I must exert myself in order to give in the same measure as I have received and am receiving."

The illusion that we are genuinely self-sufficient is one of our most tempting myths. It surfaced in the lyrics of "People," a song that enjoyed much popularity in the 1970s: "People who need people are the luckiest people in the world." The clear implication is that some people, the unlucky ones, do not need people. This is nonsense. George Bernard Shaw dismissed such fuzzy thinking with crisp impatience: "Independence? We are all dependent on one another, every one of us on earth." *All* people need people.

The festival of Passover, in a sense, is our Fourth of July, our Independence Day, the day when our ancestors were liberated from Egyptian bondage. And yet during the Seder ritual which tells the drama of the Exodus, we proclaim, "On this night we all lean." On our Independence Day we make a declaration of dependence.

We lean upon the God who conferred on us the gift of freedom, upon those who learn to cherish that freedom, upon those who lovingly and often sacrificially preserved it down the ages, upon those who today man the ramparts wherever freedom is threatened. We all lean.

And we lean upon each other for our most elementary needs. It takes some 240 people to provide us with a slice of bread. When we drink a glass of water, we lean upon chemists, plumbers, and engineers, upon the manufacturers of pipes, spigots, and chlorine, upon a whole host of people who build reservoirs, water meters, and generators.

Our colleague, the late Rabbi Morris Adler, of blessed memory, told a story in one of his sermons which, among other things, reminds us how much all people need people. The story tells of a man in Naples who could not shake off a feeling of deep depression. So he went to a doctor for help. After a thorough examination, the physician said to the patient, "There is really nothing physically wrong with you. May I suggest that you go to the theater tonight to see the great comedian Carlini? He brings laughter to huge crowds at every performance. He surely will drive away your sadness." At these words the patient burst into tears, "But doctor," he sobbed, "I am Carlini."

Two important truths leap at us from this story. The first is that suffering and pain and anguish are the common lot of all of us. One of Boris Pasternak's characters in his *Dr. Zhivago* put his finger on the human situation when he said, "It's wonderful to be alive; but why does it always hurt?" Pain has a passkey to every home in the community, even to the Royal Palace and the White House.

There is another significant element in the Carlini episode. How is he spending his time? Because he knows the taste of sadness and depression, he is devoting his life to making people laugh, to helping them forget, however briefly, the pain they are carrying. He knows the anguish of depression and he is trying to remove it from the lives of others.

I think of Carlini because Hadassah has taken as its motif, "Take my hand" – a poignant reminder of the multitudes who need someone to help them carry their burden, to relieve their suffering, to share their anguish. A telephone call, a visit, a brief note – how big these small gestures can loom in the life of a person suffering from loneliness, abandonment, or despair. There is a desperate shortage of kindness in the world.

So many of us starve for it most of the time. One doctor said recently that 90 percent of all mental illness that he has treated could have been prevented or cured by ordinary kindness. What an indictment against us! If we see a hungry man, who is so callous that he will not give him a piece of bread? But all around us, people are starving and we do not have the time or thoughtfulness or the compassion to speak a kind word, perform a gracious act, make a call, drop a line, to give bread to emaciated spirits.

Civilization, it has been said, is just a slow process in learning to be kind. The man who has not learned that lesson remains uneducated regardless of the number of diplomas on his office walls or the number of degrees that follow his signature. The man who has learned to be kind has mastered the most vital subject in life's curriculum. His formal schooling may have been meager, his familiarity with books not very intimate. If he has learned how to bring a ray of light where there is darkness, a word of cheer where spirits have been crushed by circumstances – that man is civilized. "The All Merciful desires the heart" is what our tradition tells us.

"Take my hand" and when you do, you'll be taking away my self-pity, my sense of hopelessness, my terrible feeling of aloneness. We are all Carlini and, like him, we have the capacity to bring cheer not to multitudes at once but to one solitary person at a time. And in bringing cheer to someone else, we help to give meaning to our own lives.

I recall a woman whom I encountered while I was making some hospital visits at the Albert Einstein Medical Center in Philadelphia. I knew that she was involved with many, many problems in her family, including illness and divorce.

"What are you doing here?" I asked her.

"I do volunteer work twice a week," she said.

"Where do you get the strength to do it?"

"If I didn't come here," she said, "I couldn't carry my own problems. This work keeps me going."

As she spoke, I thought of the advice that Dr. Karl Menninger gave us: "If you feel a nervous breakdown coming on, lock up your house, go across the railway tracks, find someone in need, and invest yourself in helping that person."

The poet puts this same basic truth about us in rhyme:

Man, like the graceful vine, supported lives;
The strength he gains is from the embrace he gives.

15

God so fashioned us that we are not satisfied merely to be satisfied. We have a deep-rooted craving to give satisfaction. Erich Fromm, the noted psychologist, has underlined this truth:

> Not he who has much is rich, but he who gives much. The hoarder, who is anxiously worried about losing something is, psychologically speaking, the poor impoverished man, regardless of how much he has. Whoever is capable of giving of himself is rich.

As we feed, we are fed. As we give, we receive. As we lift, we are raised. As we go out of ourselves into something bigger than ourselves, we become bigger in the process and we provide the most nourishing sustenance our craving hearts demand.

"Help your brother's boat across, and lo, your own has reached the shore."

1998/5758

The Art of Failing

In some religions, the congregants confess to their spiritual leader. On this day of confession, I would like to reverse the process by making a confession to my congregants. One of the crushing burdens of preaching, especially on these holy days, is deciding what themes are worthy of consideration when the whole family is together. Having made the decision about what to say, the problem then is how to say it. This point was driven home to me with special force recently when I read the story of the woman who acquired a great deal of wealth. Influenced by the mini-series *Roots*, she wanted to have a book written about her genealogy. So she engaged a well-known author to do it. In the course of his research, he discovered that one of her grandfathers had been executed in the electric chair in Sing-Sing. The woman tried to get the author to remove any mention of that from her biography, but he said that that would be impossible. However, one could tell it in such a way that it wouldn't hurt so much. So when the book appeared, it included these sentences. "One of her grandfathers occupied the chair of 'applied electricity' in one of America's best-known institutions. He was very attached to his position and he literally died in the harness."

The late Dr. Abraham Joshua Heschel, a master in the use of the English language, made no effort to dress up a naked truth when he spoke once to a group of rabbis about the meaning of this day. "Lies are all failures; at least one day a year we should recognize it."

Tonight I want to talk about failure – not to teach you how to fail; we all manage to do that without any help, thank you – but rather I want to think with you on how to look at failure, what to do with it, how to handle it.

Americans are success-oriented constantly. We worship what William James called the "bitch goddess success." Success is big in America, but life is filled with failure. There is so much failure, in fact, that the Massachusetts Institute of Technology (M.I.T.) has initiated a new course on failure as a dominating theme in society. To fail is an experience that we must all learn to understand and handle in order to lead any kind of life at all.

Most of us do not need any reminders about the reality of large and small failures during the course of our lives. The faculty at M.I.T. points out that a fear of failure – whether it concerns school, business, marriage, or health – dominates the American imagination. It is small wonder that some persons, catching the tide right, have made a big success out of courses, books, and seminars which promise some immunity to failure in any or all of these endeavors. "How to Succeed" are the first words of scores of book titles that have recently appeared. Helping people to avoid failure is a growth industry in the United States.

Dr. Heschel is right: we are all failures. At least one day a year we should recognize it. William Sloane Coffin, who had just been appointed to the Riverside Memorial Church to replace a successor to Fosdick, when the book *I'm O.K., You're O.K.* appeared, quipped, "I'm not O.K., you're not O.K., but that's O.K." Accept ourselves and each other with our strengths and our weaknesses, our small successes and our big failures. It's terribly important. There are a lot of lonely, friendless people because they look for perfection in friends. We must not look for perfect friends because, if they were looking for perfection, would they choose us as friends?

There's a story of a young man who was looking for many years for the perfect girl to marry. After long years and persistent searching, he found her, but alas for him, she was looking for the perfect man. So that our first truth that confronts us is that failure is very much a part of every life. A child must learn very early to realize that failing is part of living. To lead the child to believe otherwise is to deny reality and to bring him up in an atmosphere of false and destructive illusion. Eternal triumph exists only in the world of fantasy. To love your child for his achievements is easy. To love him for his failures is to love him well. It is that love that will make the later man whom failure cannot defeat.

In his book, Joshua L. Liebman quotes the story of a psychiatrist who treated one of his patients for two years for alcoholism. One day the patient appeared at the session with the news that on the day before, he had been fired from his job. "You know, doctor," he said, "if a year ago this would have happened, I wouldn't have been able to take it. I'd have gotten good and drunk. In fact, I wanted to last night but somehow I realized that if I could face this failure without terror, look at it for what it was, I'd be much better off in general. I mean that failure, just like success, is one of the great experiences. It's human."

A second truth about failure is that failure, like success, is impartial. The successful man, when you really get to know him, has a history of many failures.

Why have so many celebrated and gifted persons such as Ernest Hemingway and Marilyn Monroe and dozens of others, killed themselves at the height of their success? No one succeeds in everything, and no one fails in everything. And we must not punish ourselves by focusing so exclusively on our defeats that we lose sight of our genuine victories.

A dramatist named Alfred Sutro once wrote a fine forgotten play called *Maker of Men* in which a bank clerk returns home after missing a promotion. He says, "I see other men getting on, what have I done?" His wife answers, "You have made a woman love you. You have given me respect and admiration and loyalty, everything that a man can give his wife except luxuries – and that I don't need. Shall you call yourself a failure who, within these four walls, are the greatest success?"

Another insight into handling failure is provided by this awesome Day of Atonement itself. The message of *Yom Kippur* is that failure need never be final. That is the basic meaning of repentance, *Teshuvah*. Failure need not be final in the moral arena. Failure need not be final in any other arena of human endeavors. Much of the greatness in people is manufactured out of the raw material of failure by people who refuse to give failure the last word.

I am thinking of a 15-year-old youngster who once stood sheepishly before the headmaster of a Munich school who was reading the riot act to him. The boy was soundly censored for lack of interest in his studies and was asked to leave school. "Your presence in the class destroys the respect of the students," the headmaster scolded. The youngster took an examination to enter Federal Polytechnic School in Zurich but failed to pass. He entered another school to finish his training and then applied for an assistantship at the Polytechnic. Again, he was refused. He secured a position as a tutor for boys in a boarding house but soon was fired. Finally, he managed to obtain a job in a patent office in Berne. The man who compiled this string of failures was none other than Albert Einstein, the great teacher and mathematician. He refused to give failure the last word.

I am thinking of another man who had an impressive record of failures and defeats. He failed in business in 1831. He was defeated for the legislature in 1832. He failed again in business in 1833. His sweetheart died in 1835. He had a nervous breakdown in 1836. He was defeated for speaker in 1838. He was defeated for elector in 1840. He was defeated for Congress in 1843...defeated for Congress in 1848...defeated for the Senate in 1855...defeated for Vice President in 1856...defeated for the Senate in 1858...and elected President in 1860! His name was Abraham Lincoln. He was a man whom failure could not defeat because he would not give failure the last word.

Let us now take our theme one step further and come upon another redeeming and reassuring truth about our failures. They can be used to teach us great lessons...to leave us wiser, better, and stronger for having failed. Nietzsche said, "What does not destroy me makes me stronger."

Ernest Hemingway, in *A Farewell to Arms*, wrote, "Life breaks all of us and often many are strong in the broken places."

The professors at M.I.T. are divided on how to define "failure." Some of the faculty members have suggested that a two-part definition be used. The first is "bad," indicating those experiences that give rise to feelings of inadequacy and guilt in us. "Failure learned" describes the experiences in which, through making a mistake, we enlarge ourselves by learning something. We must try and learn from our failures.

Somebody once wrote that failures should be cremated, not embalmed. True enough. But I say they should not be cremated until we have performed an autopsy. What caused the failure? What did I do wrong? What can I learn about failure? Failure will teach us nothing and leave us none the richer if we look for scapegoats, if we try to pin the blame for our failures on others, on our heredity, on our environment, on prejudice. A man may fail many times, but he's not a failure until he says, "Somebody pushed me."

This same truth was put a little differently on the desk sign in front of a business executive: "If you could kick the person responsible for most of your troubles, you wouldn't be able to sit for six months."

To perform an autopsy on our failures, our defeats, our disappointments, means to confront them honestly, to see what we have learned from them and then venture forth again, determined to be better equipped because of what we have endured and what we have learned.

I want now to eulogize our former *shamash*. He died a few weeks before the High Holidays. He was a man who earned a great deal of love in the congregation. How did our friend, Binyamin, earn such intimate a place in so many hearts? The answer was his friendship, his compassion, his humanity, his sincerity. There was another reason I admired him so much: it was his courage. He lost his entire family – his wife and children, except for one child – in the Holocaust. And then after such a massive disaster, he went on to build a new life and a new family.

I am persuaded in my own heart that Binyamin's compounded tragedy made him more humane. And that he could honestly say along with Wordsworth, "A great distress hath humanized my soul." Binyamin was for me a constant reminder that our failures, our defeats, our heartbreaks, even they can be used to make us bigger and better human beings. They never embittered him; they never soured him. He danced the liveliest on the holiday of *Simchat Torah*. He sang the loudest when he came to our *smachot*, our personal joys. He was a person who, like the oyster, took the grit of failure and defeat and heartbreak and made of it a pearl! He left us all enriched.

To be a Jew is to belong to a people which has known more failure than any other people – slavery…burned temples…destroyed homelands…exiles…pogroms… deportations…the Holocaust. To be a Jew is to be considered as the greatest of prophets as the man Moses, who failed in his central personal mission to enter the Promised Land. Martin Buber said, "We Jews are the blood of Amos, of Jeremiah, and of all who died unsuccessfully. We know a different world history from this one, which describes its success."

Yet, in a larger sense, we have indeed been successful. We remained alive – we survived. We preserved our distinctiveness; we enriched the whole world with the gifts of our minds and spirit so that even a man like George Bernard Shaw, who, not a great friend of ours, would say, "The Jew is born civilized."

What has enabled us to succeed above the failures? It was our understanding of what it is that makes all our failures worthwhile. That we stand for something. That we possess something which is uniquely our own and supremely precious. These are the truths we must live by if our lives are to be the success that this day assures us they can be.

1975/5735

As We Think

A little while ago, at a football game in California, four or five people reported ill during a game with symptoms of food poisoning. The examining physician, trying to see whether a common factor existed, discovered upon questioning that all of them had a drink from the soft drink dispensing machine. And so he had to take into account that the syrup might have been the culprit. But then he noticed that the dispensing machine was serviced by copper piping, and that caused him to wonder whether some copper sulfate had leaked into the drink and caused the food poisoning. He felt that as an act of responsibility, all the other people in the stands who might have drunk from the same machine should be alerted to this possible danger. And so a public announcement was made, telling the people in the stands what had happened to a few people and also suggesting that they not consume any drinks from the dispensing machines until such time as the exact cause of the illness could be ascertained.

As soon as this announcement was made, the entire stadium became a sea of retching and fainting people. Ambulances from five hospitals had to ply back and forth. Two hundred persons had to be hospitalized and hundreds of others went to their own physicians with symptoms identical to those of the people who had reported ill: retching, fainting, severe abdominal pain.

But then it was ascertained that neither the water, the syrup, nor the copper pipes was responsible for the illness.

As soon as this became known, everyone became mysteriously well.

Question: How is it possible that a few words in the air could be converted into specific illness? What is it about the human mind that can process sounds into disease?

And if this is true in the case of a vagrant announcement at a football game, just imagine what happens in our daily lives when there are all sorts of words and sounds around us that produce apprehension, despair, or illness.

A second thing we have to consider is that, if words can make us ill, then words can make us better. Emotions can produce physical

23

devastation; emotions also produce the ingredients of repair, recovery, and health.

Negative emotions can produce illness. Panic, depression, frustration, rage, and hate all produce negative biochemical changes in the body. What we think, how we process our emotions, our attitudes all have something to do with how we feel.

Positive emotions produce positive physical changes. Hope, love, faith, laughter, the will to live, purpose, determination. Norman Cousins, who reported the incident at the football game, speaks with special authority. In 1964, he had helped to cure himself of a supposedly incurable disease of the connective tissues by, among other things, laughing. In *Anatomy of an Illness*, he describes his own efforts in partnership with his doctor to establish a positive frame of mind for himself by watching Marx Brothers movies and reading books by great humorists. He points out that laughter was only a metaphor for the entire range of positive emotions that he marshaled. He felt that hope, a will to live, cheerfulness, and confidence each play an important role in the therapeutic process.

Cousins is no mere amateur, idly speculating about what causes healing. As a result of the publication of his book, he was invited to join the faculty of the School of Medicine at UCLA, where he has been researching and teaching the biochemistry of emotions. His books and his experience provide great hope for the rest of us. What he affirms is that whatever happens to us in life, be it illness, disappointment, or defeat, our own attitude toward these experiences can make a major difference in our recovery. He has provided dramatic and eloquent proof of the truth our Bible long ago proclaimed:

> "A merry heart is a good medicine, but a broken spirit dries the bones." (*Proverbs* 17:22)

> "As a man thinketh in his heart so is he." (*Proverbs* 23:7)

This is a theme worth pondering at the beginning of a New Year. We usually approach it with a long shopping list – what we should like the New Year to bring us. Norman Cousins reminds us that far more crucial is what we bring to the New Year. What happens to us is, of course, important. Over that, however, we have only limited control. But more important is what we do with what happens to us – how we internalize it, assimilate it, how we process it in our minds, how we react to it. And over that we have great control because the *City of Contentment is located in the State of Mind*.

William James, the eminent American psychologist who taught at Harvard, wrote, "The greatest discovery of my generation is that human beings can alter their lives by altering their attitudes."

One of the most powerful forces that act on every one of us is the image of ourselves that we carry around with us inside our heads in our imagination. That's why we call it "imagination" – it's the part of our mind that furnishes images for us to look at.

The chief handicap that many people have is not a poor brain, but the wrong pictures of themselves which come to dominate them – poor self-image. Many are paralyzed because they are burdened with a negative self-image. They have told themselves so often, "I can't do it," that they get an image of themselves as a person who can't do things, and the image prevents them from putting forth a real effort.

We tend to become what we imagine ourselves to be. A track coach once made a pole vault man put in his room a picture of himself clearing the bar in fine form, not because he wanted the man to become conceited, but because he knew that the deciding factor in the man's performance would be the idea in the man's mind of what he could do. He wanted to make that positive image of the man doing a successful job dominant in his mind. And it worked!

What our minds can conceive and believe, we can achieve.

If we are to succeed, we must think success. If we are to be well, we must think healthful, positive thoughts. If we are to be happy, we must think happiness. "Most people," said Abraham Lincoln "are about as happy as they make up their minds to be."

Happiness does not reside in our work. It is found in our attitude towards our work. Happiness does not depend on what happens outside of us but on what happens inside of us. Happiness is not found in our possessions. It is found in how much we appreciate what we have. A tub was large enough for Diogenes but the world was too small for Alexander the Great.

In any given situation, at any given moment we have a wide range of attitudes from which to choose. If we're looking for things to complain about, none of us would have any trouble finding them. Every life is filled with an assortment of reasonable complaints about the management of the universe. But if we become fixated on the things that hurt, then life becomes a series of pains. We know the chronic complainers, and soon we find excuses for avoiding them.

On the other hand, if we are looking for things to rejoice over, then surely we will find them; and what a difference they can make in the way we feel. We become like the resident in the geriatric center when asked how she feels. "Fine," she said with a twinkle. "I have two teeth left and, thank God, they are directly opposite each other."

The role of our attitudes is reflected in the quip that whether a black cat crossing your path is bad luck depends on whether you're a man or a mouse.

Mark Twain dispensed sound advice when he counseled: "Draft your thoughts away from your troubles – by the ears, by the heels, or any other way you can manage it. It's the healthiest thing a body can do."

This is not always easy. But so much depends on it.

Someone has made a reliable estimate of things we worry about. Things that never happen – 40%. Things that are past that cannot be changed by all the worry in the world – 30%. Needless worries about our health – 12%. Petty, miscellaneous worries – 10%. Real, legitimate worries – 8%. Ninety-two percent of our worries take up valuable time, cause painful stress, and are absolutely unnecessary. And our legitimate worries…there are two kinds: problems we can solve, if we learn how, and problems beyond our ability to solve. Our attitudes penetrate every area of our lives. Our attitudes even affect our physical appearance. The fingers of our thoughts are ceaselessly molding our faces. "Beautiful thoughts make a beautiful soul and a beautiful soul makes a beautiful face." (Author unknown)

And if our thoughts cannot mold our faces, surely our attitudes towards our faces can make a difference.

Golda Meir, in Charlotte Chandler's *The Ultimate Seduction*, remarks:

> I was never a beauty. There was a time when I was
> sorry about that, when I was old enough to understand
> the importance of it and, looking in any mirror,

26

realized it was something I was never going to have. Then I found what I wanted to do in life, and being called pretty no longer had any importance.

It was only much later that I realized that *not* being beautiful was a blessing in disguise. It forced me to develop my inner resources. I came to understand that women who cannot lean on their beauty and need to make something of their own, have the advantage.

She didn't change her face. She changed her attitude towards the importance of physical attractiveness. She went further. Given the physical disadvantage she felt, she had to compensate by cultivating the spiritual qualities she possessed in such marvelous abundance.

I want to tell the story of a remarkable man, General Natan Nir. He was born in 1935 in Warsaw, into a Zionist family. His first terrible test came with the war, when he fled for his life with his mother and almost starved to death. Somehow he survived and got to Eretz Yisrael.

He dreamed of becoming a flyer but due to a heart murmur he became a tank officer.

He fought in 1956 in the Sinai Campaign. Then he commanded 44 tanks in the Six Day War in 1967. He was severely wounded in his legs. The doctors ordered amputation of both, but he refused. He insisted on surgery to save the legs. He underwent 42 operations. They saved the legs and he was left with a 75% disability. He refused a desk job and went back to a field command. He left his wife and two children temporarily in 1973 to fight in the *Yom Kippur* War and was wounded in the head and neck. And still he refused to quit!

Finally, he became a teacher of those who operated tanks. He studied in America and realized his childhood dream by learning to fly! But that was not enough. He entered politics and ran for mayor in his city, Ashkelon.

In a beautiful Chasidic story, a man dreams that he has died and gone to the "world to come." He is judged as to the quality of his earthly life, and at last, permitted to enter the celestial gates of Paradise. Much to his surprise, he finds a simple shtetl-like house of study, where he sees the greatest sages of Jewish history deeply absorbed in sacred study.

"Is this all there is?" the man exclaims. "I thought this was Paradise!"

Whereupon a heavenly voice gently informs him, "Foolish one, the sages are not in Paradise. Paradise is in the sages."

As the Maggid of Mezritch – chief disciple of the *Baal Shem Tov* – once declared, "Each person creates his own Paradise." The reverse is also true.

Dr. Aaron Beck, author of the deservedly popular *Feeling Good,* has been working with depressed people for more than twenty years. He uses a treatment system he calls "cognitive therapy," a matter of convincing the patient that neither he nor the world is as bad as he thinks. Often, these depressing ideas have accumulated over several years until they totally dominate the victim.

In the movie, *Marty*, Ernest Borgnine tells his rather plain-looking girlfriend, "You're not such a dog as you think you are and neither is the world in which you live." That's the essence of Dr. Beck's message to his patients, expressed in this poem:

> If you think you are beaten, you are;
> If you think you dare not, you don't.
> If you'd like to win, but think you can't;
> It's almost a cinch you won't.
> Life's battles don't always go to the stronger or faster man;
> But sooner or later, the man who wins is the one who thinks he can.

1990/5750

Something There

Sometime in 1983, *The Philadelphia Inquirer* carried a story about 50-year-old Jim McGowan, a paraplegic since the age of 19, who made a successful parachute jump, landing on target in the middle of Lake Wallenpaupack in the Pocono Mountains. Intrigued by this spectacular achievement, I tracked Jim down and I learned a lot of other things about him. He lives alone, cooks his own meals, cleans his own house, drives himself in his specially equipped auto, has written three books, and has taken the photographs for the first book ever published on the history of wheelchair sports.

About a week after the *Inquirer* carried Jim's story, it carried the story of another paraplegic. He was Kenneth B. Wright, a high school football star and, later, an avid wrestler, boxer, hunter, and skin diver. A broken neck sustained in a wrestling match in 1979 left him paralyzed from the chest down. He underwent therapy, and his doctors were hopeful that one day he would be able to walk with the help of braces and crutches.

But, apparently, the former athlete could not reconcile himself to his physical disability. He prevailed upon two of his best friends to take him in his wheelchair to a wooded area, where they left him alone with a 12-gauge shotgun. He held the shotgun to his abdomen and pulled the trigger. Kenneth Wright, 24, committed suicide.

In a subsequent column in the *Philadelphia Inquirer* for which I was writing, I contrasted these two paraplegics. One gave up on life; the other taught us to "say yes to life."

When the book by that name was launched at Temple Sinai, Jim flew up from Florida to share his remarkable story with us. He delivered a most moving talk which left all of us who heard it profoundly uplifted.

When I saw Jim on the pulpit again last Saturday night, I could not help but think again of the paraplegic who committed suicide. I don't mean to sit in judgment of him. Who knows what any one of us would have done in his terrible situation?

But what was his verdict when he looked at his life and at his future?

There's nothing there!

Nothing to live for, nothing to hope for, nothing to make life worthwhile.

This is a verdict a rabbi hears more often than most people. It's the cry of a bereaved parent; a very ill patient; an elderly person. What is there left for me to live for, why should I go on, how can I go on? I can't give that bereaved parent or terminally ill person any answer. Life has never tested me so cruelly. But I can point to Jim McGowan, to his victorious life and inspiring example. In a hundred ways Jim has said, "There is indeed something there!" And if you say "yes to life" and struggle patiently through the black night of despair, you will find it. To all who find themselves in a time of darkness (at one time or another, we all do) Jim's words shine with a luminous radiance: "Since I am responsible for my life, I'm going to make it as beautiful as I can."

I'm going to struggle with all my power because there is indeed something there.

1986/5746

The Valley of Decision

Of all the 150 psalms in our biblical *Book of Psalms*, the best known and the most deeply beloved is the 23rd. There we enter into the valley of the shadow of death which none can avoid.

Today I want you to come with me into another biblical valley, which provided the title of a popular novel some decades ago, Marsha Davenport's, *The Valley of Decision*. And incidentally, some forty years earlier, Edith Wharton wrote a book by the very same title. The "valley of decision" is found in an obscure verse of an obscure prophet Joel, "Multitudes, multitudes are in the valley of decision."

While the biblical reference is obscure, the valley of decision is very well known. It is not an isolated place to attract a rare visitor. It is, as the prophet said, "a gathering place for the multitudes." Indeed, we spend a very substantial part of our lives in the valley of decision. There is scarcely a day that you and I don't spend at least some of the day there. And the most crucial moments of our days may very well be precisely those moments.

Now, to be sure, some of the decisions we make day by day are about casual and trivial things. What color outfit should I wear today? What shall we have for dinner? What TV program shall we watch? Some decisions are of momentous significance. To operate or not to operate, to change jobs or to sweat it out, to hold onto our marriage, to try to make a go of it, or to throw in the dish towel, to make *aliya*, or to stay in America?

Some people find the process of decision-making of any kind extremely difficult and unbelievably painful. A recent cartoon shows a schoolboy sitting at the breakfast table surrounded by a half dozen boxes of cereal. He looks at his mother in obvious frustration and the caption says, "Decisions... decisions... decisions." An applicant for an executive position is filling out a questionnaire. He answers the questions very swiftly, but then he comes to one over which he agitates, switches, and sweats. The question asks, "Do you have trouble making decisions?" Finally he answers "yes and no."

One of the most solemn and sobering notes of the High Holy Days is struck when we are reminded that these are days of decision, when our destinies are shaped and decreed. "Who shall live and who shall die? Who shall obtain the measure of his days and who shall not obtain it?...Who shall be tranquil and who shall be disturbed? Who shall be at ease and who shall be afflicted?" These are decisions made about us over which, for the most part, we have little or no control.

But the High Holy Days speak also of those decisions that only we can make, which are totally within our control. After we enumerate all the contingencies which might befall us, we affirm immediately our power to make some extremely crucial decisions – to decide whether we shall live penitently, prayerfully, and charitably.

But I don't think it would be any distortion at all to refer to it as the *great* valley of decision. And on this day, the whole weight of the tradition, the entire power of all the generations that have gone before, the insistence of the relenting voice of God within ourselves and above us, all combine to urge us to make the kind of decisions which *Yom Kippur* symbolizes so preeminently.

Having said this, however, I would be less than honest if I did not add in the very next breath that it is not easy these days to make moral decisions. It has probably never been more difficult. Moral values have become blurred. Old values that we once took for granted are today being challenged and flaunted. Ancient institutions are being questioned and undermined. In the words of Mark Connolly, the popular playwright, "Everything nailed down is coming loose."

The Jewish Theological Seminary of America sponsors an annual Institute for Religious and Cultural Studies. This institute is open to clergymen and teachers of all denominations. A recent brochure listed the lecture topics for the year, which consisted of:

> Social revolution in America;
> Revolution in the schools;
> Revolution in the church;
> Revolution at the contemporary world phenomena; and
> Revolution and the individual clergyman.

All fifteen lectures listed for the year had the word "revolution" in the subject. Because moral values have become blurred, immoral behavior has proliferated. In the year that both the president and the vice president of our country left office under black clouds of scandal, it is not easy to call upon the citizen to listen to ancient preachments when he stands in his own valley of decision.

We ought to note at this point that the Jew who lives by his tradition, the Jew who is guided in his daily actions by Torah and a Jewish standard of decency, has many compensations. Not the least of them is the fact that he spends very little time in the valley of moral decisions. He doesn't have to sweat every day whether or not he should be honest or truthful or responsible or faithful. These decisions have been made a long time ago. And he is bound as a committed Jew to shape his behavior by the *mitzvot* and the Commandments. To be sure, he is subject to temptation no less than everybody else around him. But his problem is not *what* is right. His problem is: "Do I have the strength to do that which is right?" But for those who would not accept what has been handed down as their exclusive guide to behavior, who day by day must enter into the valley of moral decision in a ruthless economy, in a competitive society, in an age of uncertain guideposts and disappearing landmarks, is there any help that we can offer when they find themselves in the valley of moral decision?

I should like to suggest, dear friends, four questions that we ought to ask ourselves before we make the moral decision. The first question is: "Can the decision I make stand the test of publicity? What if everybody knew what I am going to do? This decision about which I am uncertain, does it need secrecy? Does it require a cover-up? Suppose our family and our friends knew about it."

I believe that this is a very penetrating test to which to submit a contemplated decision. One thing we can be very sure of – if it requires a cover-up, it cannot bring any contentment or peace of mind; it will cost more than it is worth. The words of Phillips Brooks should be recorded and taken to heart:

> To keep clear of concealment...to do nothing which might not be done on The Middle of Boston Common at noonday...I cannot say how more and more that seems to me to be the glory of a person's life. It is an awful hour when the personal necessity of hiding anything comes...the whole life is different thereafter. Where there are questions to be feared, and eyes to be avoided, and subjects which must not be touched, then

the bloom of life is gone. Put off that day as long as possible. Put it off forever if you can.

Let us make sure then, in the first place, that our contemplated action can pass the test of publicity.

When we stand in the valley of moral decision we should ask ourselves a second question: "Will my *best* self approve the contemplated course of action?" I stress the words *best* self because the fact is that we are each very complicated and very complex. It would be much easier to make a moral decision if each one of us was a single self, but the fact is that we are each a bundle of many selves. There is a thoughtful self and a selfish one. There is a gentle self and a cruel one. There is one that is concerned only with the immediate gratification, and the one that pays attention to ultimate principle.

There was a dramatic illustration of our moral ambivalence in the newspaper just two weeks ago. A certain Mr. Jackson was picked up by the police. He was charged with eleven murders over the last several years. The woman with whom he had been living told the police that "Jack was the kind of person that, if you needed something and he had it, he'd give it to you." She recalled that "Once while walking along Broadway, a dude who looked like he just got out of a garbage can came up and asked Jack for a dollar." She said it was Jack's last dollar but he gave it to him. That's how good he was. This is the same man who was picked up for the murder of some eleven people!

The poet, Goethe, said in one of his epigrams that it was regrettable that nature had made only one man, since there was material enough for at least two people – a rogue and a gentleman.

Do you remember the story of the woman who laid her case before Alexander the Great? When he handed down the decision, she was greatly displeased and exclaimed, "Your majesty, I appeal."

"You appeal?" asked Alexander, astonished. "How can you appeal? I am the highest authority of the realm."

Whereupon the woman answered softly, "I appeal from Alexander the Small to Alexander the Great."

When we stand in the valley of moral decision, the action that we contemplate should be the one that appeals to the great one within us, to our best and highest self.

When we stand in the valley of moral decision, we must ask ourselves a third question before we embark upon a course of action: "Where does this action lead? What are its likely consequences?"

Long ago, our sages taught, "*Ezeh hu chacham? Haroeh et hanolad.*" "Who is wise? He who sees the consequences of his deed." He understands that when we pick up one end of a stick, we are at the same time picking up the other end. When we choose one end of the road, we are also choosing the other end of the road. Every course of behavior has a place where it begins and a place where it comes out. Those who play bridge and read the columns are often given this very sound advice by experts: "Watch out how you play for the first trick." But often the bridge player plays that first card without thinking, and then he discovers to his dismay that he has already lost the contract. A deliberate pause before that first card was thrown could have made all the difference.

Professor Sol Lieberman in our seminary once drew a perceptive distinction between a wise man and a clever man. "A clever man," he said, "knows how to get out of a situation that a wise man would not have gotten into in the first place." We rely too much on our cleverness when we should be guided by wisdom. And wisdom asks, "Where does this course of action lead to?" "*Ezeh hu chacham? Haroeh et hanolad.*"

The last question we might ask ourselves when we stand in the valley of moral decision is: "What if everybody did what we are contemplating doing? What kind of society would it be? What kind of *world* would it be? If everybody acted precisely as we are thinking of acting? Would the world be a brighter or shabbier place in which to live if our action became the norm, the guide, the universal?"

Do you remember the story of the Chelemites, those citizens of the legendary community of Chelm who were not overly endowed with intelligence? They decided to have a huge celebration on *Simchat Torah.* There would be wine and merriment for all. But being a poor community, there were no funds available for the wine. Whereupon they decided that each Chelemite would bring to the party a quart of wine. And they would pour the individual contributions into the community barrel "*and es vet zine fraylach*"– they would make merry. One Chelemite, who was a real *chacham*, said to himself, "I will bring water. After all, if everybody brings wine, how much will it really matter if I bring water?" The night of the party, when the spigot of the community barrel was opened, what flowed out was nice, fresh water! Every Chelemite had the same original thought. If everybody brought to the community barrel what we are contemplating bringing, what would there be – wine or water?

One of the most beautiful prescriptions for living is found in the words of a wise man who advised, "Be such a man and live such a life that if every man were such as you and every life like yours, this earth would be God's paradise." Intelligence is the capacity to choose between, to make a choice. The glory and the anguish of being human flows from this capacity to choose between alternative courses of action, to make moral decisions. At a time when our society faces moral problems of unprecedented dimensions, each of us has an obligation to ask, "Am I part of the problem, or am I part of the solution?" And each of us, according to the tradition, must view the world in a breathless state of balance, with our next action the decisive one, the one which will tilt the scales for good or for evil. In the valley of decision, each of us stands in awesome solitude. But our actions can reach to the farthest ends of the universe.

Let us choose a life that needs no cover-up or concealment. A life which merits the approval of the best, of the highest within us. A life whose consequences bring joy and fulfillment. A life which can serve as a model to others, who walk by our side, for those who will remain after us.

1974/5734

LOSS

Finding God in Great Loss

For more than a half-century, I was a provider of comfort. As the rabbi of a congregation with a large membership, I officiated regularly at funerals, delivered eulogies, and ministered to the mourners in their grief.

Many of the sermons I preached and printed were designed to offer comfort and guidance. I took seriously the message of Isaiah, "Comfort, oh comfort my people, says your God."

And then a harsh blow created a complete role reversal. The death of our gifted daughter, Shira, after a brief bout with cancer, left me desperately in need of comfort. Only other parents who have walked this road can fully understand the bitter anguish of burying a child. As her simple pine casket was being lowered into the grave, I had to suppress a fierce desire to cry out, "This is crazy! This is not the way it is supposed to be! I should not be burying her; she should be burying me."

The thud of the coffin meeting the bottom of the grave was the exclamation mark that answered all unscreamed protests. That's the way it is. The grave will soon be filled with earth embracing her lifeless body, and we will go home with empty, aching hearts.

The ride back to Shira and John's home in Manhattan to observe *shiva*, the first seven days of mourning, was not as long as the heavy ride to the cemetery. We reflected on the funeral service, which had overflowed the sanctuary of the Society for the Advancement of Judaism.

Two of the speakers who had an enormous impact on the audience were a couple whom Shira had counseled when they were dealing with their five-year-old daughter's cancer. The husband said:

> The process of dealing with our daughter's death, while appalling and shattering, also was full of beauty, and full of love, our family facing the approach of death together. ...Shira facilitated that. ...Shira was a radiant force for understanding and for growth.

38

His wife added, "I felt lifted by Shira. Almost immediately I thought, 'Ah, at last we have been found. We have been heard.'"

These and other immense tributes unloosed floods of tears. What a privilege to be Shira's father. At her birth, we had given her two Hebrew names, *Shira Brachah*. They mean *song* and *blessing*. The names were prophetic.

Another source of comfort for the entire family was the service held three times a day in her home for the seven days (exclusive of our Sabbath) following the interment. I found reciting the *Kaddish* at each service exceedingly consoling. While the *Kaddish* is called "the mourner's prayer," it contains not a word about death or the dead. The *Kaddish* is, from beginning to end, a hymn of praise to God. Thanking God at a time of a grievous loss? At such a time, we are more likely to harbor complaints against the management of the universe. The garment of faith often shrinks in the waters of adversity. And yet, and yet…say *Kaddish*, insists an ancient, wise tradition.

Even as I recite the words, I think of why I should be grateful. I take a quick inventory of the blessings Shira brought into our lives.

I am grateful beyond words that she loved her life so deeply. In her eulogy, her dear friend, Peppi, recounted a telephone call she received from Shira late at night about two weeks before her death. "Peppi," she said, "I'm not going to *Olam haba* ("the world to come," a Hebrew synonym for heaven). I'm not going to *Olam haba* because I have had *Olam haba* right here." Terminal cancer and all, she felt extravagantly blessed.

We also derived great comfort from the hundreds of people who extended condolences and performed acts of generosity and charity in Shira's memory. The massive evidence of human kindness was overwhelming and humbling.

In recent days, I have been asked more than once: "As a rabbi, is your faith in God shaken? Do you still believe in God in the face of this terrible loss?"

No glib answer will do. I never believed, nor do I now believe, that faith in God is a guarantee that no misfortune will befall the believer, that tragedy will visit others but not me or mine. How could I? My mother died at age 39 when I was 11. Two brothers were a little older. Our sister was four. And I have consoled too many bereaved believers.

Sorrow has a passkey to every home, and cancer is very democratic. Where, then, is God when tragedy strikes?

God, for me, was in the compassion and kindness shown to us by so many people.

God was in the amazing strength that was given to us in our heavy pilgrimage through the valley of the shadow of death.

God was in the healing that is binding our wounds ever so slowly but ever so surely. God was in the extraordinary gift Shira embodied.

God is in the power of memory to keep Shira a living reality in our hearts, minds, and souls.

God is in our sustaining conviction that death is not a period that brings the sentence of life to a full stop; it is only a comma that punctuates it to loftier significance.

This is the faith that burst forth out of Emerson after the death of his young son: "What is excellent, as God lives, is permanent." We come from God and we return to God, and with the Source of life, each soul is lovingly safe.

1998/5759

Losses

On Rosh Hashanah, we are confronted by the uncertainty of life.
On Yom Kippur, especially at Yizkor time, we are confronted by the certainty of death.

On Rosh Hashanah, we focus on those blessings we should like to receive.
At Yizkor time, we recall the loved ones we have lost.

On Rosh Hashanah, we might well review our achievements and accomplishments of the days that have come and gone, and gratefully calculate our gains.
At this particular moment before Yizkor, our thoughts are more likely to be riveted on our losses.

***

Loss, as we surely know, is an inevitable part of life. And it is not only death that inflicts loss upon us.

A few months ago, Judith Viorst lectured in Philadelphia. Judith Viorst is a graduate of the Washington Psychoanalytic Institute and the author of several entertaining and instructive best sellers, including *How Did I Get to be Forty – and Other Atrocities*, and *It's Hard to be Hip Over Thirty – and Other Tragedies of Married Life*. The subject of her lecture was the theme of what is probably her best-known book, *Necessary Losses*. If you haven't read the book, I suggest you read it. If you have read it, I suggest you do what I did – read it again. It is a wise book, delightfully written, persuasively argued. It is ripe with guidance, deep in understanding, full of compassion for our human condition.

The subtitle of the book sums up her argument in *Necessary Losses – The Loves, The Illusions, The Dependencies, and Impossible Expectations That All Of Us Have to Give Up in Order to Grow*. She reminds us that:

41

We begin life with loss. We are cast from the womb without an apartment, a charge plate, a job, or a car. We are sucking, sobbing, clinging, helpless babies. Our mother interposes herself between us and the world, protecting us from overwhelming anxiety. We have no greater need than this need for our mother.

Babies need mothers. Sometimes lawyers, housewives, pilots, writers, and electricians also need mothers. For the presence of mother, our mother, stands for safety. Fear of her loss is the earliest terror we know. "There is no such thing as a baby," writes psychoanalyst and pediatrician D.W. Winnicott, observing that babies in fact can't exist without mothers. Separation anxiety derives from the literal truth that without a care-taking presence we would die.

In the early years of life, we embark on the process of giving up what we have to give up to be separate human beings. But until we learn to tolerate our physical and psychological separateness, our need for our mother's presence – our mother's literal, actual presence – is absolute.

It's hard to become a separate self, to separate both literally and emotionally, to be able to outwardly stand alone and to inwardly feel ourselves to be distinct. There are losses we'll have to sustain, though they may be balanced by our gains, as we move away from the body and being of our mother. But if our mother leaves us when we are too young, too unprepared, too scared, or too helpless, the cost of this leaving, the cost of this loss, the cost of this separation may be too high. There is a time to separate from our mother. But unless we are ready to separate, unless we are ready to leave and be left, anything is better than separation.

Loss then extends beyond the loss of people we love. It is a far more encompassing theme in our lives. For we lose not only through death but also by leaving and being left, by changing and letting go and moving on. Our losses include not only our separations and departures from those we love. There are our conscious and unconscious losses of romantic dreams, illusions of freedom and power, and impossible expectations.

The great Jewish humorist, Sam Levenson, in describing the Jewish American experience, once wrote:

> My folks were immigrants and they fell under the spell of the American legend that the streets of America were paved with gold. When my father got here, though, he found out three things. First, we saw that the streets were not paved with gold. The second thing he noticed was that the streets were not even paved, and last but not least, he discovered that he was the one who was expected to do the paving.

There are also our illusions of safety and the loss of our own younger self – the self that thought it always would be unwrinkled, invulnerable, and immortal.

Somewhat wrinkled, highly vulnerable, and mortal, we become inescapably aware of losses, these life-long losses, these necessary losses. We confront these losses when we are confronted by the towering fact that…

Our mother is going to leave us, and we will leave her;

Our mother's love can never be ours alone;

What hurts us cannot always be kissed and made better;

We are essentially out here on our own;

We will have to accept, in other people and in ourselves, the intermingling of love with hate, of the good with the bad;

Our options are constricted by nature and nurture;

There are flaws in every human connection, relationship;

Our status on this planet is irreversibly impermanent, temporary;

43

We are utterly powerless to offer ourselves or those we love protection;

We cannot offer protection from danger and pain, from the inroads of time, from the coming of age, from the coming of death – protection from our necessary losses.

These losses are a part of life – universal, unavoidable, inexorable. And these losses are necessary because we grow by losing and leaving and letting go.

There is a vital bond between our losses and gains. For the road to human development is paved with renunciation. Throughout our lives we grow by giving up. We give up some of our deepest attachments to others. We give up certain cherished parts of ourselves. We must confront, in the dreams we dream, as well as in our intimate relationships, all that we never will have and never will be. Passionate investment leaves us vulnerable to loss. There is a high cost of loving and sometimes, no matter how clever we are, we must lose. All love stories have unhappy endings.

C.S. Lewis wrote in *The Four Loves*:

Love anything and your heart will be wrung and possibly broken. If you want to make sure of keeping it intact you must give it to no one, not even an animal. Wrap it carefully round with hobbies and little luxuries; avoid all entanglements. Lock it up safe in the casket or coffin of your selfishness. But in that casket – safe, dark, motionless, airless – it will change. It will not be broken; it will become unbreakable, impenetrable, irredeemable. To love is to be vulnerable.

In *Cinema Paradiso* (which means "beautiful film"), Old Alfredo, who possesses the special wisdom not uncommon among the illiterate, says to his very young and mischievous friend, Toto, "You will learn that life is not like it is in the movies."

At any age we would surely agree that loss tends to be difficult and painful. But it is only through our losses that we become fully developed human beings. The archer hits his target partly by pulling, partly by letting go. The boatman reaches land partly by pulling, partly by letting go.

Central to understanding our lives is understanding how we deal with loss. The people we are and the lives we lead are determined for better or worse by our losses – how we handle them, how we go on after them.

In speaking about necessary losses at *Yizkor* time, I'd like to be faithful to the other themes of this day – atonement, repentance, forgiveness – by focusing also on the losses that are not inevitable; on unnecessary losses.

This dimension of our theme is suggested by a series of cartoons that hold up a mirror to our predicament. As you know, I find great truth in cartoons. You also know that "Ziggy" is my special fount of wisdom. Ziggy comes to a lost and found section in a department store and says, "I lost the courage of my convictions."

In another cartoon, "The Better Half," the husband is in bed and his wife, in curlers and robe, is standing at the bed somewhat disturbed. "Tell my boss I'm staying home to attend a funeral. My ambition died."

How many of us have lost heart? Lost loyalty to our Jewish way of life? Face? Self-esteem? Self-respect? Hope?

Yom Kippur assures us that we can regain these unnecessary losses. We cannot bring back loved ones. We cannot bring back our youth, our illusions, our impossible expectations. We can recover our unnecessary losses – our courage, ambition, self-esteem, self-respect, hope.

Here Judith Viorst offers some reassurance that although we are driven by forces that are beyond our control and awareness, we are also the active authors of our fate. And that, although the course of our lives is marked with repetition and continuity, it also is remarkably open to change. She writes:

> For yes, it is true that as long as we live we may keep
> repeating the patterns established in childhood. It is
> true that the present is powerfully shaped by the past.

45

But it also is true that the circumstances of every stage of development can shake up and revise the old arrangements. And it's true that insight at any age can free us from singing the same sad songs again.

Thus, although our early experiences are decisive, some of these decisions can be reversed. We can't understand our history in terms of continuity or change. We must include both.

1991/5751

Lessons in a Hospital Bed

Many years ago when I was working on my first book, *A Treasury of Comfort*, I came across a statement that came back to me uninvited when I found myself, quite unexpectedly, in Room 6H17 in Abington Hospital. The statement, as I recall it, went like this: "God sometimes puts us on our back so that we might look up to Him." As these words seemed now to be speaking directly to me, I asked myself whether that was the explanation for the stroke that came like a thief in the middle of the first night after our return from a rather strenuous trip to Israel.

I don't propose to be able to read God's mind. (Sometimes I hope He can't read mine, either.) But lying in a hospital bed most assuredly directed my focus upward and frankly, I thought of God more in Room 6H17 than I probably do when I lie down at night in the comfort and security of my own home.

What was I thinking when I looked up to God? My dominant feelings were not complaints about the management of the universe, especially as it related to one of God's "chosen" servants who covers his Dresher, Pennsylvania territory for Him. One question that I fiercely resisted was, "Why me?" Too often I have tried strenuously to dissuade others from whining that self-pitying question. Strange as it may sound, I say in all honesty that my overwhelming feeling was a feeling of deep gratitude.

Gratitude, you ask? Yes, indeed. Gratitude for more blessings than I can either count or deserve.

Gratitude for this amazing body which has served me so long, so well, and has responded uncomplainingly to the myriad and frequently unreasonable demands I have made upon it.

Gratitude for the mildness of the stroke which left me virtually unimpaired, able to tie my own shoes, button my own shirt, comb my hair, shave my face, think logical thoughts, and speak distinctly and coherently. (Do we normally consider the multiple miracles that each of these "simple" acts requires? Is it to remind us of this simple evasive truth that we thank God three times each day in the silent devotion "for Your miracles which are daily with us evening, morn,

and noon and for Your wonders and kindnesses at every moment?")
One doctor friend said I had "a lucky stroke."

Gratitude for the good community-minded people who build
hospitals and the dedicated souls who become physicians and nurses
to minister to the stricken and to the ailing.

Gratitude for the overwhelming Niagara of prayers and good
wishes, acts of generosity and charity that my illness precipitated.

Gratitude for the Temple Sinai family whose love was so
palpable I could taste it.

Gratitude for my awareness that my invisible roommate was
the Almighty Himself, who according to the psalmist promised, "He
will call to Me and I will answer him. I will be with him in distress
and I will rescue him."

When I wound my *tefillin* around my sleepy left arm in my
hospital room, I was aware of the biblical verse that tells us why we
bind the *tefillin* around the arm: "Because with an outstretched arm I
brought forth the children of Israel out of Egypt." That arm with the
tefillin said to me, "If God could take the children of Israel out of
Egypt, He could bring me home from Room 6H17."

Yes, when I looked up to Him I could only think of the words
of the patriarch Jacob in a moment of dread and foreboding: "I am
unworthy of all the kindnesses and all the mercies You have shown to
Your servant."

From my hospital room I called a congregant who, I learned,
was also hospitalized. When I told him where I was calling from and
why I was there, he exclaimed, "You, of all people!" He had
obviously succumbed to the myth surrounding a rabbi. Somehow the
rabbi is supposed to be invulnerable, out of the reach of sorrow,
misfortune, and illness. But illness and trouble are great democrats.
They spare no one. They have a passkey to every home. And
sometimes even the rabbi has to learn that humbling lesson. His body
cannot be overtaxed with impunity. The body takes revenge for
repeated slights.

Our daughter, Shira, kept sermonizing, "Listen to your body."
I asked myself, "Am I Exhibit A of her preaching?" I *am* grateful for
that lesson, although the tuition was a little high and I could have used
a little less dramatic illustration of its truth.

I am hopeful that the week I spent in the hospital bed has given me greater empathy for the occupants of the many hospital beds I visit, and perhaps I will be able to bring to the sick a greater measure of comfort because I was so recently there.

I cannot conclude this litany of blessings without including a special word of deepest thanksgiving to my many colleagues from near and far who expressed their concern, their prayers, and warm wishes. I was especially heartened by the Chancellor of the Jewish Theological Seminary of America, Dr. Ismar Schorsch, who took the time to write a most generous note of encouragement. I am abidingly grateful to him.

Special emotional and spiritual therapy came in a box of letters and homemade, self-decorated cards from the kids in our Hebrew school and pre-school. Here are some of the pills and vitamins their colorful cards delivered:

> Roses are red,
> Violets are blue.
> The Torah is sweet and so are you.

> Roses are red,
> Violets are blue.
> You're in bed, but at least you're not dead.

(Come to think of it, that's no small consolation).

Urgent motivation for a speedy recovery was found in the following note:

> Dear Rabbi,
> I hope you can come back soon. One week ago we got a new dog and named him Nugget. I would like you to find him a Hebrew name.

Several of the cards expressed the hope that I will be home in time for the Super Bowl. I made it. But as a former New Yorker and a natural rooter for the Buffalo Bills, I could have done without it. I hope that game did not seriously retard my recovery.

For last, I have left what is dearest to me: my family – Hilda, the kids, their kids, and the various branches of the family tree – provided boundless love and warm fuzzies. At this time, the family, which is so easily overlooked when things are serene, assumed central and crucial significance in my recovery. There are no words to convey what my family has meant to me in this time of need.

I am grateful, too, for learning once more the greatness of little things. The heart-melting impact of small acts of concern, caring, and kindness. What a difference they make in the complexion of the moment and the day. What a big lift a small act of love can give to a drooping spirit.

So in brief, yes, I did look up to Him, but I did not grumble. I was too grateful for the power He gave to each of us to reach out in love and friendship, to share in each other's pain, to rejoice in each other's happiness, to care and to comfort, to be able in time of trouble to look up to Him in faith and thus regain our will and strength to live.

1980/5740

We Are All One Family

It is a melancholy coincidence that I should be given this heavy honor of memorializing colleagues and wives of colleagues at a time when I am observing the *yahrzeit* of our daughter, Shira, which occurs three days from today, and on Thursday, I am going to mark the *yahrzeit* of my mother, who died when I was eleven. Why was I given the heavy honor of doing this portion of our program of our coming together? I am sure that the chairman who assigned me this very special place didn't know of these *yahrzeits* that were converging.

This multiple memorial that we're conducting here today has become commonplace in our time, when the grisly work of the terrorists brings multiple sorrows. In a sense, they bring together those who are the victims of their malevolence. Israel and America are united today as never before. Some people believe that the terrorists hate America because of Israel. Yet, as Benjamin Netanyahu pointed out in his speech before the Congress of the United States, the truth is the other way around. The terrorists hate Israel because of America. America, in their terminology and in their ideology is the "Big Satan"; Israel is the "Little Satan."

And I think it is a melancholy coincidence that the blackest days on the calendars of America and Israel are classified by dates. *Tisha B'av,* the 9th of *Av*, 9/11, no name, just a date, just numbers. There is no name vile enough to capture the cruelty. And put the two nines together, we get *chai.* The determination of the enemies of America and Israel to wipe us out only strengthens our resolve to live. "On the day that the Temple was destroyed, the Messiah was born." "I shall not die but I shall live and declare God's work."

I don't know how many of us know the name of Rabbi David Suissa, the founder of a magazine called *OLAM*. It's a beautiful magazine. He said something that is very important. Referring to 9/11, he said, "We all feel like we're family members of the victims of 9/11." We all feel like we are family members in bereavement.

Hilda and I visited Israel in 1967 right after the Six Day War, when the Rabbinical Assembly had planned a pilgrimage to Israel for the rabbis and their wives. We were there coincidentally on that

51

pilgrimage. Those of us who were there will recall that the mood in Israel at that time was unbridled euphoria. Israel had looked into the jaws of death and emerged not only alive but victorious. On the streets of Jerusalem, people would stop soldiers and hug them and kiss them. You cannot begin to imagine how that population responded to that victory. And when we came back to our congregation, we shared with our people to the extent that words could convey this extraordinary experience. We gave them some intimation of what was going on in Israel. Apparently we did it effectively enough that they asked us to lead a pilgrimage of Temple Sinai people to Israel. We did it then, and the next year, and for the next dozen years.

I remember one visit in particular. As some of us know, *Yom Haatzmaut*, Independence Day in Israel, is preceded by *Yom Hazikaron*, Remembrance Day. Israel pauses to remember those who made that independence possible, those who purchased it with their young blood.

One *Yom Hazikaron* stands out in my mind:

Golda Meir, who was then the Prime Minister, addressed an audience at the Mann Auditorium. Attendance was restricted to families who had lost loved ones in Israel's wars. Somehow, because we had brought the group of American tourists, we were granted permission to attend this gathering on *Yom Hazikaron.* And in the auditorium filled with mourners, we were wondering what this wise lady was going to say. I remember those heavy words with which she began. She uttered each word as though it weighed 100 pounds and was carved out of her heart. She began, "*Kulanu b'nai mishpachah achat anachnu.* (We are all members of one family)."

When we read the names of our colleagues and the lovely wives of rabbis, don't we feel in our bones the words of Golda Meir, "*Kulanu b'nai mishpachah achat anachnu*" – we are all mourners? We are all bereft. We are all diminished. Our sages teach us that "*chacham sh'met hakol krovov.*" When a wise man dies, all are his relatives. Those colleagues who died are part of our family. To be a relative means to feel more pain. I think we each feel a deep pain over the death of a colleague because there is a special relationship between rabbis and rabbis more than there is between dermatologists and dermatologists or chiropodists and chiropodists. We are literally in the same work. And what one colleague accomplishes brings glory to himself and sheds the glory over all of us. And if God forbid the reverse happens, it is also true. So we do indeed have an added measure of pain. In no other profession are people who practice it as close to one another and involved with one another as rabbis are with each other.

I remember that, on one of our anniversaries at Temple Sinai, I told the story of the rabbi in a small town who had trouble sleeping one particular night. He got up and dressed himself in peasant clothes and walked through the town. He met the night watchman who did not recognize him because he was not in rabbinic garb. They walked together silently in the loneliness of the night. After a while the rabbi said to the night watchman, whom he didn't know, "Whom do you work for?" The night watchman explained that he worked for the township. They pay him to keep walking around the town to make sure things are safe, so that the people could sleep securely. They continued walking silently. And then the night watchman turned to the rabbi and asked, "Whom do you work for?" The rabbi didn't answer right away and they kept walking.

After a while the rabbi turned to the night watchman and said, "How much do you get for your work as a night watchman?" "I get 25 rubles a month." The rabbi said to him, "Come and work for me. I'll pay you more." The night watchman said, "What will be my duties working for you?" Said the rabbi, "Your duties are going to be very simple. Once every day you have to ask me, 'Whom do you work for?'"

Well, dear friends, whom do we work for? I asked my congregants, whom do we work for? I work for Temple Sinai. Whom does Temple Sinai work for? The United Synagogue. Whom does The United Synagogue work for? For Conservative Judaism. Whom does Conservative Judaism work for?

When we prepare to take the Torah from the Ark we proclaim, "*Ana avda d'Kudshah brich hu.*" "I am the servant of the Holy One Blessed Be He." That's whom we work for. "*Ana avda d'Kudshah brich hu.*" That's whom we all work for. Isn't it true? One of the reasons why I loved my congregants is that they also worked for the same boss. I didn't work for them. Whom did they work for? Whom did I work for? I got paid for what I did. They didn't get paid. They gave their service on their television time, their reading time, their family time. Whom do we work for? "I am the Servant of the Holy One Blessed Be He..." A neighboring rabbi who is Reform or Orthodox or Lubavitch, whom does he work for? The same God. The same people. The same Torah. And if he makes the same rabbi beloved in the hearts of his people, don't I get the benefit of that love, too? And when his son marries my daughter, they both love the same God, the same people, the same tradition, aren't they going to perpetuate what I work for, what he works for? We are all members of one family. And so when we lose a colleague, we lose literally a co-worker in the cause in which we are enlisted body and soul. And when a *rebetzin* dies, a member of our family has been taken from us. The *rebetzin* is more involved in the work of her husband than the wife of any other professional that I can think of.

So when we remember these people, the people who worked alongside of us, for us, and for the very things for which we have dedicated our lives, we remember members of our own family. We remember all the people whose lives have touched our own, those who have blessed us and those who have bruised us, those who have uplifted us and those who have depressed us. They're with us all the time. We use those years again and again. Our years are recycled. We have to ask ourselves, "Am I living in the way that my years will be worth reliving?" "*Kulanu b'nai mishpachah achat ananachnu.*" We are all members of one family. And death brings us closer together.

Thornton Wilder, in his moving story "Our Town," revealed a profound truth when he wrote, "There are two lands, the land of the living and the land of the dead, and the bridge is love." Those of us who have lost loved ones – and I don't think anyone here falls outside of that category – we know that the bridge of love is one which we travel regularly, frequently.

An old Jewish legend says that when a good man dies, an angel comes and puts on his closed eyelids the Hebrew letter *tuf.* Some people believe that the letter *tuf* was chosen because it's the last letter of the Hebrew alphabet, as though to say that the last word has been spoken, the last chapter has been written. It's the end of the story. But I believe the letter *tuf* stands for *tichyeh* (you shall live). We believe that, don't we? We believe that profoundly. We believe it, especially when we have to say goodbye to somebody so very, very dear to us. *Tichyeh.* You shall live.

A little while ago, Hilda and I attended a healing session for those who have lost loved ones, and there they read something by Rabbi Naomi Levy – *The Teachings of the Broken Pieces.* Just as our forebears carried the broken pieces of the first Ten Commandments in the Ark of the Covenant, we too carry the broken pieces of our and others' life stories with us. We shall never forget that these broken pieces are often our greatest teachers. From them we learn our strengths. We learn compassion, wisdom, understanding, devotion, faith, and insightful personal growth. From them we learn how to pray, how to cry, how to listen, and how to reach out for help. It is from them that we learn how to strive for better, how to empathize and offer help. And then she wrote this prayer:

> My wounds may heal, God, but my scars may never
> fade.
> Help me to embrace them, not despise them.
> Teach me how to live with my broken pieces, how to
> tend to them, how to learn from them.
> Remind me that I possess the power to turn my curses
> into blessings, my shame into pride, my sadness into
> strength, my pain into compassion.

The rabbi whom I consider to have been the most brilliant rabbi to ever step into a pulpit before a loudspeaker was Milton Steinberg. The most humanizing sermon he wrote, as far as I'm concerned, was included in my anthology *A Treasury of Comfort.* The sermon is called "To Hold with Open Arms." If you haven't read it, read it. If you've read it, read it again. It will enrich you. This is what he said, in part:

> For these things are not and never have been mine,
> they belong to the universe and to the God who stands
> behind it. True I have been privileged to enjoy them
> for an hour. But they were always a loan due to be
> recalled and I let go of them willingly because I know
> that they are part of the divine economy that will not

be lost. The sunset, the bird's song, the baby's smile, the thunder of music, the surge of great poetry, the dreams of the heart of my own being, dear to me as every man's life is to him, all these I can trust well to Him who made them. There's a poignancy and regret on giving them up but no anxiety. When they slip from my hands they will pass to hands better, stronger and wiser than mine.

On November 6, 1995, President Clinton spoke at the funeral of Yitzhak Rabin. Part of what he said at that time could be a source of comfort to us at this time. As Moses said to the Children of Israel, when he knew he would not cross over to the Promised Land, "Be strong and of good courage. Fear not, for God will go with you. He will not fail you. He will not forsake you."

Last night I was having a little trouble falling asleep. I suddenly remembered Hilda's father. He was born in Kolomea and, whenever he met a landsman who came to his dental office to be treated, he would greet him with these Yiddish words: "*Abee men zeyht zich.*" "As long as we see one another."

I think that the magnet that draws us to these conferences is not that we expect to hear great sermons or great insights. We've heard them all in our time. But, "*abee men zeyht zich.*" We come to see and be seen. Isn't that true? And then we come to this conference and a good friend, a colleague, says, "Sidney, I'm going blind. I have macular degeneration." "*Abee men zeyht zich?*" When will we see each other again? And then you have an assignment to call the roll of those who won't be here anymore, those who aren't here anymore. "*Abee men zeyht zich.*" As long as we see each other.

Let us embrace those whom we do see and those who share with us, knowing that life is brief, that we all work for the same boss, and that we are all part of the same family.

May I conclude by offering a prayer I wrote for one of the prayer books I co-edited:

May the memories of our loved ones inspire us
To seek in our lives those qualities of mind and heart
Which we recall with special gratitude.

May we help to bring closer to fulfillment
Their highest ideals and noblest strivings.

May the memories of our loved ones deepen our loyalty
To that which cannot die –
Our faith, our love, and our devotion to our heritage.

As we ponder life's transience and frailty,
Help us, O God, to use each precious moment wisely,
To fill each day with all the compassion and kindness
Which You have placed within our reach.

Thus will the memories of our loved ones abide among us
As a source of undying inspiration and enduring blessing.

1999/5759

Rabbi Sidney Greenberg

GROWTH AND RENEWAL

Rabbi Greenberg Remembers

When I was asked to add a personal entry to our archives, I thought long and hard about the nature of my contribution. I finally decided to go back to the very beginning of my rabbinate in order to examine some of the conditions that prevailed in 1942, and some of the feelings that I shared with the congregation at that time. The remarks that follow are excerpts from my installation address in November of that year, the year it all began for me.

There are moments when one becomes painfully aware of the inadequacy of words to convey sentiments and ideas that crave and merit expression and yet, at the same time, elude it. Such a moment is mine now. I am overwhelmed by intimate feelings too deep to be translated into words, and stirring thoughts too numerous to be captured. But difficult as it may be to properly express these feelings, it is even more difficult to suppress them. And so the attempt, however feeble, must be made.

I am filled with a feeling of humility that is prompted not only by the realization that I owe so much to so many, but by the additional awareness of the magnitude of the task of being a rabbi. It is a great and exacting task, fraught with massive responsibility. Even a Moses pleads incompetence when offered the mantle of leadership. And our sages in the Talmud rather bluntly and realistically revealed the true implications of spiritual leadership when they pictured God as saying to the leaders of the Jewish people, "Do you think that it is only a position of glory and honor which I have given to you? I have in fact given you servitude." Yes, it is servitude – servitude on behalf of our people and our people's faith.

If that was true in the past, how much truer is it today? In a world reeling under the impact of catastrophe, the lot of the Jew is especially bitter. A haunting fear possesses every reader of the Anglo-Jewish press every time he picks up a newspaper copy, for he knows that it will contain another brutal chapter in the grim story of Nazi wanton destruction of Jewish life. I am sometimes selfishly grateful for the stark injustice the American press does our people by omitting or silently passing over the reports of hundreds of thousands of Jews butchered in Europe. A constant reminder of the full measure of our misery would undermine hope and courage. Yet such is the extent of the breach of our people.

Our tradition teaches that when Jacob was fleeing from the wrath of his brother Esau, "The whole world became like a stone wall on his path." How true that is today. The whole world has become a veritable stone wall before us. Even the Eternal road has been closed. Escape through migration is no longer possible for the vast majority.

In these terribly trying times, the rabbi's task is especially trying. It is to the healing of this tremendous physical breach that the rabbi today has to dedicate himself. Upon him evolves the difficult duty to maintain his own courage and to transmit to his people a firm faith at a very dark time. He must be able to preach the message of hope.

Despite the darkness of the moment, tomorrow will come "and in the morning you shall see the glory of the Lord." Despite the heartache and grief of today, tomorrow the Lord will wipe away all tears. Despite the frustrations of the present hour, despite the fears and anxieties, the rabbi, like the prophet of old, must be able to preach out of the depth of his own desperate convictions: "Comfort ye, comfort ye my people, saith your God. …For behold darkness shall cover the earth and gross darkness the peoples; but upon you the Lord will arise and His glory shall be seen upon you." It is therefore to the healing of this physical breach that the rabbi today has to enslave himself.

And it is also to the healing of the spiritual breach of his people that the rabbi must consecrate himself. It is a sad thought indeed, that what thousands of years of frightful persecutions could not take away from us – our Judaism – we in America are giving away freely. The apathy and indifference of American Jews are too well known to warrant description. To overcome that indifference is indeed a heroic task. And the rabbi must labor with determined dedication to ideals that permit no compromise. He cannot say, as one politician is reported to have said at the end of a campaign speech, "Fellow citizens, these are my sentiments, but if they don't suit you they can be changed." The rabbi must speak out on behalf of Divine imperatives of which he is the custodian. The teachings that he must

61

convey may not always fall pleasantly upon his congregation's ears, but he must be able to say without flinching, "Thus says the Lord."

Perhaps our sages were justified in debating whether the priests in the ancient Temple in Jerusalem were messengers of God or messengers of the people. But where the rabbi is concerned, there can be no distinction. The rabbi must be both. He must act in a dual capacity. Even while he bears the responsibility of his congregation, he is burdened with the unyielding message of God. In fact, he cannot truly fulfill his obligations to his people unless he is a messenger of God. How challenging is God's admonition to the prophet Ezekiel: "Son of man, I have set you a watchman to the house of Israel; therefore, when you shall hear the word of My mouth, warn them from Me. Yes, I give you servitude."

I welcome that servitude now and I am humbly grateful for the opportunity to labor in the vineyard of the Lord. If the responsibility is great, the rewards are greater. But I shall need your assistance and the inspiration that only your cooperation can bring.

Our sages tell us that during the years in the desert when God was angry with Israel, He did not speak to Moses. No spiritual leader can receive Divine guidance when his people alienate God and forsake His teachings. We must advance together towards our common goals, and together, we can go on from our modest beginnings to make of Temple Sinai a house of God that will reflect honor upon its members and upon all Israel.

Much, very much, still remains to be done. We are heartened, however, by the fact that we have come a long way in a short time. I know that we are yet too young to indulge in the luxury of reminiscence. But it is always good psychology when plodding up a steep hill, when the path ahead seems too difficult, to cast a glance over one's shoulder and derive strength to carry on by scanning the distance already covered. From the backward glance comes vision and faith for the future. With that faith, we shall toil until the promise of Job's friend shall be true of us: "Though your beginnings are small, your end shall be very great."

And so, it is in a spirit of genuine gratitude and self-dedication that I pray:

May it be Your will, O God, that I shall not stumble in my teachings, that I shall not mislead my people, and that my friends and colleagues shall not be ashamed of me. Teach me, O God, what I shall say, make me to understand what I shall speak.

1947/5707

Covering Our Sackcloths

It was a period of profound crisis for Samaria, the capital of the northern kingdom of ancient Israel. The King of Aram and his armies had besieged the city and its inhabitants were being starved to death. So intense had the hunger become that mothers began to devour their young. When this news reached the king of Israel, the Bible tells us, "He rent his clothes…and the people looked and behold, he had sackcloth within upon his flesh."

What a shock that sight must have been to the people! Each citizen knew of his personal troubles and tragedies. But how amazed they all must have been to see that beneath his royal robe, even the king was wearing a sackcloth – the symbol of personal sorrow and misfortune.

A deep truth speaks out to us from this incident, one that we ought to keep steadily before us, especially in time of trouble. "Why did this happen to me?" people frequently ask the rabbi amidst sorrow, as though they alone were singled out by a malicious destiny, as a target for its bitter shafts. We rarely stop to realize that even kings wear sackcloths.

The better I get to know people, the more impressed do I become with this one fact. Rare indeed is the individual without a sackcloth. Some of us wear the sackcloth of a deep frustration – a career to which we aspired but did not attain, a heart we sought but failed to win. Some of us wear the sackcloth of a haunting sense of inadequacy, or a deeply bruised conscience, or an aching void left by the passing of a loved one. Blasted hopes, unrealized dreams, anguish and grief – is any life unfamiliar with them? Is not the sackcloth the common garment of all?

There is a second significance to the biblical incident. The king wore his sackcloth *underneath.* He did not make of it his outer garment. He did not display it too prominently, either to others or to himself. Here was an act of wisdom we would do well to emulate.

Fathers and mothers have sustained grievous losses during the past few years. Ours has been the tragic generation of which our sages spoke – the generation where parents bury children. Doubly tragic are

64

those afflicted parents who have not learned to cover their sackcloths, who have made of it their outer garment.

In this matter, the rituals of Judaism concerning mourning contain an excellent prescription for emotional recovery from misfortune. Judaism prescribes a terminus to mourning. Just as it is a law that the *Kaddish* must be said for eleven months, so is it a law that the *Kaddish* may not be recited longer than eleven months. The *shiva* period may likewise not be prolonged beyond seven days. After *shiva*, the mourners must leave their sorrow-laden homes and go out into the healing sunshine of human society. After the prescribed period of mourning, the sackcloth must become an undergarment.

Some time ago, the widow of Colin Kelly was remarried. To some, her remarriage appeared as an act of disloyalty to the memory of her husband. In defense of what she had done, she said quite simply: "Of course you can never forget the past and the past will always color the present. But I do not think that you should let the past affect the present so much that there can be no future." This is an attitude that can usefully be applied to every sackcloth that life imposes. We must never let the past affect the present so much that there can be no future. If life is to be lived at all, we must learn to cover our sackcloths. But with what shall we cover them?

The first thing we can use to cover our sackcloths, it seems to me, is the "Robe of Understanding." We tend to regard trouble as an intruder, an interloper who has no place in life's scheme of things. In the words of a popular song, we often think that the world was made only for fun and frolic. Nothing makes the wearing of life's sackcloths more difficult to endure than the fact that we are not prepared for them.

If we would learn to wear life's sackcloths properly we must cover them with the "Robe of Understanding." We must realize that, as the Bible puts it, "Man is born to trouble." Trouble, far from being a gatecrasher in life's arena, actually has a reserved seat there. Human life is attended at its beginning by the piercing cries of the infant and at its end by the agonized wailing of the bereaved. In between, there are sadness, heartbreak, and disease. For that reason, the great tragedians of literature have not wanted for themes. All they had to do was to observe life carefully and report it faithfully, and the tragedy spelled itself out. "Man is born to trouble."

I know that many will feel that such a gloomy view of life leads to pessimism and despair. Actually, however, the reverse is true. If we accept realistically life's somber backdrop, then the manifold blessings we enjoy will emerge in bolder relief. The love which nourishes us, the friendship which warms us, the beauty which inspires us, the health which sustains us – all these and the countless other blessings which are ours will be all the more gratefully welcomed.

God grant us the "Robe of Understanding" to cover our sackcloths.

But the "Robe of Understanding," beautiful and becoming as it is, is not enough. For at best it can only teach us the spirit of resignation to our troubles, and it is not enough to merely *accept* trouble; we must do more. We must learn to *use* trouble and convert it into a stepping-stone to triumph. For that we need the "Robe of Wisdom."

In the 48th chapter of the *Book of Isaiah*, there is a very remarkable verse. The prophet is chastising his people, and among other things, he says to them, according to Moffat's translation, "I purged you, but nothing came of it, testing you in the furnace but all in vain." Here the prophet is rebuking his people for having been through the furnace of affliction and having learned nothing from the experience: "What," he is asking them, "have you to show for all the suffering you experienced? The tragedy is not that you endured pain; the tragedy is that your pain was wasted, leaving you none the wiser, none the better."

Yes, the prophet expected his people to do more than *accept* trouble. He expected them to *use* it. The fact is that some of life's most valuable lessons can be and have been learned precisely in the crucible of adversity. We discern most clearly many a basic truth of life when our eyes are dimmed by tears. Robert Browning Hamilton expressed a common human reaction when he wrote:

> I walked a mile with Pleasure
> She chattered all the way
> But left me none the wiser
> For all she had to say.

I walked a mile with Sorrow
And ne'er a word said she
But oh the things I learned from her
When Sorrow walked with me.

We speak very often of *"victims* of circumstance"– people whose souls are crushed beneath the wheels of unfortunate events. We would do well to start thinking of *"victors* of circumstance"– people who use even negative circumstance and distill from it some new insight into life, keener understanding, or more beautiful character. We often speak of people who were successful because they knew how to take advantage of good "breaks." We would do well to start thinking that people can be successful if they have the wisdom to capitalize on their bad "breaks." It is possible to be like Wordsworth's "Happy Warrior":

Who doomed to go in company with Pain
And Fear, and Bloodshed, miserable train!
Turns his necessity to glorious gain.

Or as the Psalmist puts it:

They pass through a valley of tears and
convert it into a life-giving fountain.

God grant us the "Robe of Wisdom" to cover our sackcloths.

Thirdly, may God grant us the "Robe of Wisdom" to cover our sackcloths with the "Robe of Service." There is a legend of a sorrowing woman who came to a wise man with the heartrending plea that he return to her her only son whom she had just lost. He told her that he could comply with her request on one condition: she would have to bring to him a mustard seed taken from a home entirely free from sorrow. The woman set out on her quest. Years elapsed and she did not return. One day the wise man chanced upon her, but he hardly recognized her. Now she looked so radiant. He greeted her and then asked her why she had never kept their appointment. "Oh," she said in a tone of voice indicating that she had completely forgotten about it. "Well, this is what happened. In search of the mustard seed, I came into homes so burdened with sorrow and trouble that I just could not walk out. Who better than I could understand how heavy was the burden they bore? Who better than I could offer them the sympathy they needed? So I stayed on in each home as long as I could be of service. And," she added apologetically, "please do not be angry, but I never again thought about our appointment."

Here is a most profound truth to remember when life makes us don a sackcloth: trouble and sorrow naturally make us think only of ourselves. But after the first impact of the blow has worn off, our emotional recovery depends upon our ability to forget ourselves. And there is no better way of forgetting about ourselves than by thinking of and serving others. Human experience every day confirms the truth of the legend. He who can do no better after sorrow than engage in the futile search for the mustard seed to restore the loss, which is in fact irretrievable, is destined to spend years of avoidable heartache. But happy is he who can rise from his mourner's bench and so lose himself in the service of others that he finds himself unknowingly climbing the mountain of healing to which the road of service inevitably leads.

Man like the clinging vine supported lives.
The strength he gains is from the embrace he gives.

God grant us the "Robe of Service" to cover our sackcloths.

The last and most significant robe with which we might cover our sackcloths is the "Robe of Faith" – faith in the immortality of the souls of our beloved.

The *Yizkor* prayer, which is recited four times every year, makes a bold affirmation about the human soul. It declares that death has no dominion over it. "May God remember the soul of my mother…" "May God remember the soul of my son…" The soul survives to be remembered. It does not perish with the death of the body. This same faith is echoed in the "*El Male Rahamim*" prayer, where we speak of the soul as being bound up in "the bond of life everlasting." Thus Judaism, like all great religions, teaches that death is not a period that brings the sentence of life to a full stop. It is only a comma that punctuates it to loftier existence. Here is the most comforting of all robes to cover the sackcloth of bereavement.

To be sure, like all daring affirmations of Judaism, the belief in immortality cannot be scientifically demonstrated. It is as the philosopher Santayana correctly called it: "the Soul's invincible surmise." But if it is a "surmise," it is one of mankind's most persistent surmises. From ancient man in his primitive beliefs down through the long corridors of time stretching into the present, most sophisticated faiths, men have always held the human soul indestructible. Nor has this belief been limited to religious thinkers alone. Philosophers, poets, physicians, scientists, all answer "present" when the roll is called among the believers that death is not the end. How the soul *survives* is, of course, a mystery. It is no less a mystery, however, than how the soul *arrives.* It originates with the Source of all Life and flows back to its origin.

When death robs us of a loved one the pain of parting can be assuaged through our faith that the essence of our beloved lives on not only in our hearts and in our memories but more especially with the Author of Life Himself. It is this faith which burst forth from Emerson after the passing of his little son. "What is excellent," he wrote in his "Threnody," "as God lives, is permanent." It is this faith which James Whitcomb Riley summed up in his beautiful poem, "Away":

I cannot say, and I will not say
That he is dead! He is just away!

With a cheery smile, and a wave of the hand,
He has wandered into an unknown land.

And left us dreaming how very fair
It must be, since he lingers there.

And you – O you, who the wildest yearn
For the old-time step and the glad return.

Think of him faring on, as dear
In the love of There as the love of Here.

Think of him still as the same, I say;
He is not dead – he is just away!

God grant us the "Robe of Faith" to cover our sackcloths.

The story of a king introduced our problem. The story of another monarch will sum up our solution. Alexander the Great, it is told, once commissioned an artist to paint his portrait. He gave him only two conditions. It was to be an exact likeness, unfalsified. Moreover, it was to be handsome and attractive. The artist had no easy task, for over his right eye, Alexander had a prominent battle scar. The artist was thus confronted with a painful dilemma. To omit the scar would be a violation of the first condition. To include it would be a violation of the second. Finally, the artist came up with the solution. He painted Alexander in a pensive mood, his face supported by his right hand with his forefinger covering the scar.

We cannot eliminate life's scars upon our souls, for we would not be true to life. Nor can we permit them to be prominently viewed, for they would then make life ugly and unlivable.

We must learn to cover the scars upon our souls, the sackcloths upon our flesh...

With the "Robe of Understanding" which teaches us to accept trouble as part of the price we pay for being human;

With the "Robe of Wisdom" which helps us *use* trouble, and convert it into triumph;

With the "Robe of Service" which enables us to recover our own strength while at the same time bringing strength to others;

With the "Robe of Faith" which whispers comforting assurance that the soul is mightier than death.

With these robes, let us cover our sackcloths and thus make the portrait of our lives beautiful and inspiring to behold.

1980/5740

Using Other People's Years

The newspapers reported a little while ago that a high school senior who learned that he was dying of leukemia drew up a will. He listed his few possessions and he bequeathed each of them to someone especially dear to him. His most touching legacy was to his closest friend. "Dear Bob," he wrote, "Use my years also."

These are terrible times when we wish we could do just that – bequeath unlived years. The heartrending cry that so often comes from the anguished lips of a parent echoes the words of King David: "Oh my son, Absalom! Oh my son, my son Absalom! If only I had died instead of you! Oh Absalom my son, my son!" (*II Samuel* 19:1).

But of course, we cannot bequeath unlived years. If years were transferable, no child would ever die. Parents would guarantee that. Friends and loved ones can do many things for the sick. By kindness, caring, and nourishing love, they can sometimes even prolong life itself, but not by transferring years from their own "life account."

There is, however, a way in which we can and do use other people's years. Not the years they did not live but the years they did live.

"Each man," said Oliver Wendell Holmes, "is an omnibus in which all his ancestors ride." We are the product of all those lives which have touched and entered our own – parents and grandparents, brothers and sisters, teachers and friends, those who have bruised us and betrayed us, those who have sustained and strengthened us, those who added to our burdens, and those who were to us a blessing. We do use other people's years, too, because no man is an island – apart, separate, isolated.

Now, just as we use the years of those who have gone before us, our years will be used by those who come after us. This puts an added responsibility on us. "It's my life," we protest. "I can do with it as I see fit." Not quite. Our lives, our values, our goals, overflow into the lives of others – minute by minute, hour by hour, day by day.

This truth is illustrated by every autobiography. Chaim Nachman Bialik was considered, until his death in 1934, the Hebrew poet laureate. In one of his very touching poems, "Shirati," he tries to trace to its origin the sigh, the *krechtz*, which is so frequently heard in his poems. And he tells us how, in his childhood, his widowed mother would slave in the marketplace by day and toil with her domestic chores at home late into the night. Long after she thought all her children were asleep, she would be up, sewing and baking. Little Chaim in his bed overheard her unanswered protests to the Almighty, and could virtually hear her tears rolling into the dough that she was kneading for tomorrow's bread. When she served her family the warm bread on the following morning, Bialik says, he ate it and with it there entered into his bones his mother's tears and her sighs. Unbeknownst to her, of course, she was making decisive imprints on little Chaim's scroll of life that no subsequent experience could eradicate.

1989/5749

The Greatest Sin

An eighteenth-century Hasidic teacher, Rebbe Shlomo of Karlin, one day asked his pupils an intriguing question: "Which is the most grievous sin a Jew can commit?"

A number of answers were suggested. "Murder," said one. "Idolatry," said a second. "Apostasy," ventured a third. The Rebbe shook his head after each answer. After all the pupils' answers had been rejected, the Rebbe answered his own question. "The most grievous sin a Jew can commit is to forget the biblical teaching, "You are the children of the Lord your God" (*Deuteronomy* 14:1). We must never forget who we are. We are each a child of God."

It is so easy to forget this towering truth in the twentieth century.

Will Rogers, in a sarcastic comment on the well-known verse in the Eighth Psalm, once quipped, "God made man a little lower than the angels and he has been getting a little lower and lower and lower ever since."

Jean Paul Sartre, the high priest of existentialism, calls man "The incommensurable idiot of the universe."

Another modern writer, pitting himself directly against the biblical view of man declared, "There is no more divinity to man than there is to a baboon or to a speck of dust."

George Bernard Shaw's view of man was also cosmic miles from the view of Rebbe Shlomo. "Our earth," said Shaw, "is the lunatic asylum for some other planet."

Such views of man are not isolated voices of cynical hecklers shouting off stage. They have the leading role and occupy center stage in the contemporary scene.

In an age of inflation, when the price of all commodities has been spiraling, man alone has been suffering deflation, from a shrinkage in value and worth. Read contemporary literature, look at current movies and television, and see how cheap human life has become, how man's value and stature have shrunk.

And so the ancient teaching of the Hebrew Bible has been cynically revised to say, "Do unto others as others would do unto you, but you do it to them first."

We Jews have our own special difficulties in believing that man is a child of God. The wounds of the Holocaust still bleed, and too many of us had relatives whose skin was used as lamp shades, whose hair was made into mattress stuffing, and whose bodies were converted into soap. Were the murderers also children of God?

And yet, the words of Rebbe Shlomo of Karlin ring insistently in our ears. We must not forget who we are. In the first place, to look upon ourselves as the children of God is to invest our lives with their fullest potentiality.

What we think of ourselves has a powerful impact on what we make of ourselves. Convince a child that he is bad and he will become a bad child. That verdict becomes a self-fulfilling prophecy. The child grows into the image that has been projected on him. He lives up to our low expectations.

If Sartre convinces me that I am "the incommensurable idiot of the universe," then what can you expect from an idiot? If I am persuaded that I have no more divinity than a baboon or a speck of dust, then what can you expect from a baboon? If our earth is indeed merely a lunatic asylum, then what can you expect from a lunatic? We achieve as we believe!

But, if we see ourselves as God's children, then we dare not place any ceiling on human attainment. We each have boundless resources of mind and spirit waiting to be tapped, imprisoned splendor waiting to be released, vast potential waiting to become real. To see ourselves as children of God is to remove all ceilings. Morally and spiritually, the sky's the limit!

We can become more responsive to truth, more sensitive to another's pain, more capable of forgiveness, more receptive to criticism, more convinced of our capacity to grow into that more humane person we are each capable of becoming.

In *Hamlet*, Shakespeare wrote: "We know what we are, but we know not what we may be." Rebbe Shlomo would put it a little differently. "When we truly know who we are, who will dare to set a limit on what we may grow to be?"

1982/5742

The Freedom to Choose Life

An old story tells of a jury foreman who announced to the court the verdict, "Not guilty." The incredulous judge, outraged by the decision, challenged the foreman: "Why was the defendant found not guilty?"

"By reason of insanity," answered the foreman. To which the unappeased judge exclaimed, "All twelve of you?"

This story came to mind naturally enough when John W. Hinckley, Jr. was declared not guilty by reason of insanity when he shot and wounded the President and three other innocent people. The widespread sense of outrage that greeted this decision raised serious questions about the state of justice and the law in our country.

The verdict also stirred up anew an old theological question. Do you and I enjoy freedom of will to make rational choices and act accordingly, or are our deeds predetermined by some powers or influences which control and manipulate us?

In a public forum, a woman recently put this question to Isaac Bashevis Singer, Nobel Prize winner for his masterful Yiddish stories: "Do you believe," she asked, "in free will or predestination?" "That's a very easy question," he retorted with delicious irony. "We have to believe in free will. We have no choice."

We do indeed have a choice. We can choose to believe that there is no free will and that we human beings have no choice; that we are the victims of circumstances we are powerless to shape, or control.

The efforts to deny human beings free will began long ago and continue down to our own times. The ancient pagan religions taught that man was eternally doomed for having slain some god or another. Hinduism chained man to Karma, the wheel of irreversible fate. Islam pictured man's destiny as controlled by Kismet.

In modern times, behaviorists have taught that we are controlled by our environment, we are captives of our genes, our reflexes, our glands. The philosophies which would deny us freedom of will were neatly captured in the *Rubaiyat of Omar Khayyam*.

Life's but a checkerboard of nights and days
Where Destiny with Men for Pieces plays:
Hither and thither moves and mates and slays,
And one by one back in the closet lays.

Yes, we can choose not to believe in free will, but when we do so the consequences for our lives are profoundly destructive. If everything is predestined and preordained, what point is there to human initiative? Why try to change our lives or circumstances when the shape of things to be is in no way responsive to our efforts, however vigorous or well intentioned? How can we be held morally responsible for our actions when those actions are the products of forces not of our making?

Of course we can deny free will, but, as Singer indicated in his paradoxical way, when we do so we pay an awesome price. We strip ourselves of our most distinctive human endowment – the power to choose.

One of the most pernicious offenses perpetrated by the cults is their insidious use of brainwashing techniques by which they rob their members of the power to choose.

It is worth noting that the word "intelligent" is derived from two Latin words: "inter" and "legere." "Inter" means between, and "legere" means to choose. The gift of intelligence is precisely the power to choose between alternative modes of action and behavior, confident that our choices always make a significant and often decisive difference.

One day in 1870, a year after he received his medical degree from Harvard, William James read an essay by Charles Bernard Renouvier, a brilliant French social scientist and philosopher. In that essay, Renouvier wrote that "free will is the root not only of moral life but also of intellectual life and no certainty is ever attainable without it."

These words were to mark a turning point in James' life. "My first act of free will," he said, "shall be to believe in free will." Miraculously, the fears and the depression from which he had been suffering began to leave him, his pains subsided, and he took control of himself. By 1873, he began his teaching career at Harvard which was to last for 34 years and he was to become America's greatest pioneer psychologist.

When we affirm human freedom of will, we liberate ourselves to make the choices which shape our own inner world, and often even the world around us. We become free to choose compassion over cruelty, hope over despair, cooperation over combat, forgiveness over vengeance, generosity over selfishness, love over hate, and often even health over sickness.

We have no choice. We must believe in free will, in the human power to choose. When we are tempted to succumb to a sense of human impotence, the words of Dr. Victor Frankel can renew our resolve to hold fast:

> We who have lived in concentration camps can remember the men who walked through the huts comforting others, giving away their last piece of bread. They may have been few in number, but they offer sufficient proof that everything can be taken from man but one thing: the last of the human freedoms – to choose one's attitude in any given set of circumstances – to choose one's own way.

Long ago, the Bible put the challenge to us most directly. "Behold I have set before you this day, the blessing and the curse, life and death. And you shall choose life."

1981/5741

ISRAEL

Holocaust

In recent years, a melancholy observance has been added to the Jewish calendar: Yom Hashoah – Holocaust Day. On the Jewish calendar tonight, the 27th day of Nisan, we mark the unspeakable tragedy of the murder of the Six Million.

The Holocaust is not an event which we recall without pain. To invoke the memories of those who perished in the gas chambers, in the ovens, and in the mass graves is to reopen wounds that have not yet healed. It is to raise unanswerable questions about man and God.

But we must remember the Six Million. That is the very least we owe them, the immortality which remembrance confers. We are their refuge against oblivion. If we do not remember them, they die a second time. As we remember them we deny Hitler a posthumous victory.

On the wall of the entrance to Yad Vashem, the overpowering Holocaust memorial in Jerusalem, are inscribed these words by Abraham Shlonsky:

> I vow to remember as long as I live. Forgiveness to me
> is lost as an art. I promise not to unlearn and later
> regret. But to inscribe and remember all that I saw.

We must remember the Six Million for their sake and not least for our own sake. There are two things it seems that we can do. In the first place, we need more Jews. We need larger Jewish families. To all young people still planning their families, we say in the words of Gloria Goldreich, "Every Jewish baby that is born is a slap in Hitler's face."

In addition to needing more Jews, we need better Jews. That means every one of us. With more than one-third of our people destroyed, we must each take upon ourselves an added measure of responsibility. The prayers they might have offered we must offer. The books they might have created and read, we must create and read. The Shabbat candles they would have kindled, we must kindle. The *tzedakah* that they would have given, we must give every day in every way. We must be more devout, more devoted, more dedicated.

Our honored dead could not save their own lives, but if we truly remember them, they may be able to save and to deepen our lives.

1998/5778

What the Headlines Don't Tell Us

Are you in the mood to take a brief quiz on this week's Torah portion? If so, here are two questions: How many children did Adam and Eve have? What were their names?

If your answer to the first question was "two," I regret to tell you that you are wrong. If your answer to the second was "Cain and Abel," I am sorry once again to say that your answer was insufficient.

If you check *Genesis* 4:25, you will find that Adam and Eve had a third son named Seth. If you check *Genesis* 5:4, you will read that after the birth of Seth, Adam "begot sons and daughters."

If your answers were incorrect, don't feel too badly. I suspect that 95 percent of the readers gave the same answers you did. Why? Why do we all know about Cain and Abel but are unaware of the existence of their brother, Seth, and their other brothers and sisters?

The answer, I suspect, is because Cain and Abel were involved in a sensational murder case. They made the headlines and were the topic of lots of lurid conversation. But Seth and his other brothers and sisters went through life as decent, upright citizens, obeyed the laws of society, and were guilty of no acts of violence. They were therefore among the Bible's most forgettable characters.

This excursion into Bibleland is prompted in large measure by the thoughts associated with the name, "Israel," today. Say "Israel" and immediately we think of problems. That's the impression we get from our newspapers, radio, and TV.

So let's take a look at some of the unsensational aspects of Israeli life which don't make headlines and which the TV networks have apparently not found dramatic enough to attract commercial sponsors:

The first worldwide nuclear medicine conference was held in Israel in tribute to the extraordinary research by Israeli scientists in that new and vital field.

Israel is a major exporter and producer of the lifesaving CT scan device used in the most advanced hospitals in the world.

A group of visiting American judges in Israel, including blacks and Hispanics, inspected Israel's legal system and later announced that Israel is one of the most free, most democratic, most idealistic countries they had ever seen.

The Arabs who live in Israel enjoy far more democracy, greater literacy, more prosperity, better health, and longer life than the Arabs in any Arab country in the Middle East.

Three leading textile plants in the southern part of the United States have concluded a deal with an Israeli solar energy company to install an advanced solar energy system that will enable the American firms to do without oil.

During one two-month period, the Hadassah Hospital in Jerusalem treated 160 patients from Jordan, one from Iraq, thirty from Kuwait, eighteen from Saudi Arabia. Of the 356 open-heart operations done in that hospital each year, a third are on Arab patients.

According to UNESCO figures, Israel ranks second in the world in the number of books published in proportion to its population.

Israel has twelve orchestras. Of these, three or four are regarded as among the best in the world.

More than 50,000 people from some 103 countries, many of whom have no diplomatic relations with Israel, have come to that tiny country to learn teaching, farming, and how to fight disease and hunger.

Israel has developed the drip method of crop irrigation that is a substantial contribution to solving the world's urgent need for food, while conserving its limited water resources.

In 1958, a United Nations Committee of agricultural experts visited Israel and concluded that it would take twenty-five years until Israel would be able to double its agricultural production. In twenty-five years, Israel increased the production twelve-fold.

Israel already leads the world in the number of scientists and engineers involved in research and development – thirty per 10,000 population. (The U.S. is second, with twenty-five.)

Israeli scientists publish more original work in international scientific journals than any other nation, 10.2 per 20,000 population. (The U.S. is second, with 9.0.)

Israel's theater attendance per capita is the highest in the world.

None of the above items, chosen at random and severely limited by space considerations, is likely to attract a TV documentary. Or maybe, just maybe, there is some sensitive spirit in the American media who feels we owe something to that spunky, beleaguered ally that has demonstrated to all of us that even a little nation can achieve greatness.

1985/5745

Thirtieth Anniversary of the
United Nations Vote to Partition Palestine

In a speech delivered at Notre Dame University in 1955, Abba Eban made this striking observation. "Within a single lifetime we have passed from a world in which the existence of an independent Israel seemed inconceivable into a world which seems inconceivable without its existence."

The single most dramatic event which led to the creation of an independent State of Israel occurred 30 years ago today. On November 29, 1947, the United Nations voted to partition Palestine into two states, one Arab and the other Jewish.

The amount of territory allocated to the Jewish State was but a fraction of what had been promised in the Balfour Declaration some 30 years earlier. But the Jewish community accepted the partition decision because it would at last establish a sovereign Jewish State. Here the battered remnants of the Holocaust would find shelter. Here every Jew would be welcome. Here the Jewish people would carve their own destiny.

When word of the United Nations' action was broadcast to the world, Jews everywhere wept and rejoiced. The impossible dream of centuries had come true. At last the Jews had a home of their own in the ancient homeland. The greatest love story in history, the romance of a people with a land, was to be consummated with the blessing of the world.

Amidst the rejoicing, however, there was also trembling. The Arab States rejected the partition plan as they had threatened they would. On November 24, 1947, Jamal Husseini, the spokesman of the Palestine Arab Higher Committee, told the United Nations, "The partition line proposed shall be nothing but a line of fire and blood."

The Arabs kept their word. As soon as the partition resolution was passed, they began their war to prevent its implementation. In the first few hours after the passage of the resolution, they killed seven Jews. By the end of the first week, there were 105 Jewish dead. Roads were mined, convoys ambushed, settlements isolated. Thirty-five Hebrew University students were massacred on the road near Jerusalem. A convoy on the road to the Hadassah Hospital on Mount

Scopus was attacked. Seventy-seven Jewish doctors, nurses, and scientists lost their lives.

All this was but a prelude to the war that broke out in earnest on May 15, 1948 when the British Mandate over Palestine officially came to an end. The departure of the British was a signal to seven Arab states to invade the newborn State of Israel, fully expecting to liquidate the Jewish state and to drive the Israelis into the sea. On May 15, Azzam Pasha, Secretary General of the Arab League, said in Cairo, "This will be a war of extermination and a momentous massacre which will be spoken of like the Mongolian massacres and the crusades." In the War of Independence, which Israel was forced to fight, the newborn state suffered enormous casualties. A community of 650,000 people counted 6,000 dead – but tiny Israel refused to be liquidated. It refused to be swept into the sea. In the most massive display of courage of modern times, Israel, virtually unarmed, was able to beat back the invading armies with their vastly superior armies and equipment.

In the last thirty years Israel has been compelled to fight for its very survival in four additional wars. Despite these repeated assaults, Israel has managed to remain the only democratic state in that entire part of the world. Israel has become the most technically advanced country in the Middle East. She has absorbed over a million Jews from every corner of the globe, including more than a half million refugees from Arab lands. Israel has drained swamps, clothed barren hills with green, and even made the desert bloom. One can only imagine what Israel might have accomplished if its Arab neighbors had likewise accepted the partition plan.

On this anniversary, it might be well to reaffirm the words taken from Israel's Proclamation of Independence of May 14, 1948:

> We extend the hand of peace and good-neighborliness to all the States around us and to their peoples, and we call upon them to cooperate in mutual helpfulness with the independent Jewish nation in its Land. The State of Israel is prepared to make its contribution in a concerted effort for the advancement of the entire Middle East.

1978/5738

The Sin of Silence

Time has a nasty way of betraying ancient adages. A glaring victim of the passing years has been the proverb so popular in my childhood, "Speech is silver; silence is gold." The shameful silence of the civilized world in the face of the Holocaust has gone a long way towards tarnishing the gold of silence.

Today we are much more persuaded by the compelling urgency found in the words of the Swiss philosopher, Henri Frederic Amiel, who said, "Truth is not only violated by falsehood; it may be equally outraged by silence."

One who felt keenly the outrage perpetrated by silence, Martin Luther King, spoke out of the depths of his people's agony when he said, "It may well be that the greatest tragedy of this period of social transition is not the glaring noisiness of the so-called 'bad people,' but the appalling silence of the so-called 'good people.'"

The above reflections were triggered by recent events in the Middle East. One of the most painful aftermaths of Israel's attack upon the Arab planes in the Beirut airport was the message of condolence sent by the Vatican to the President of Lebanon. Shortly thereafter, the Pope gave an unprecedented interview to a leading Italian newspaper, and in the course of his remarks, he termed the Beirut raid "a black day."

The reaction within Israel to these comments from the Vatican were understandably bitter. Israel wanted to know why there had been no message of condolence sent to the President of Israel when a terrorist grenade wounded scores of innocent people at the Tomb of the Patriarchs in Hebron. Why was there no letter of condolence to Israel when a terrorist bomb was exploded in the heart of Jerusalem, killing twelve men, women, and children and wounding another fifty-three? Why was there no message of sympathy when Arab terrorists killed an Israeli engineer on an El Al airplane in Athens – the assault, incidentally, which Israel answered in Beirut?

Nor was it only Jews in Israel who were shocked by the Papal silence. The following lines appeared in a letter in the *Jerusalem Post*:

As an Israeli Catholic, I wish to condemn the message of condolence sent by the Pope to the Lebanese President after the retaliatory raid on Beirut airport. I find it impossible to understand why my spiritual leader attaches more importance to the loss of aircraft than to the loss of Israeli life by criminal Arab aggression. I have written to the Pope expressing these feelings and suggested that a message of sympathy to our President would be more justifiable.

Israel's open criticism of the Papal silence apparently did not go unnoticed or unheeded. Within a few days after it was voiced, a statement was issued by the Vatican indicating that there was Papal grief for all acts of violence. Even more reassuring was the swift message of condemnation issued by Pope Paul VI in response to the obscene and barbaric hangings in the public square of Baghdad.

Silence is not always golden. Sometimes it is yellow with cowardice. Sometimes it is gray with indifference, and frequently it is tainted with bigotry.

The sinister and corroding effect of silence in the face of moral outrages that require denunciation is also evident on the American scene. There has been mounting concern within the American-Jewish community over the outright anti-Semitic utterances and actions by black extremists. To be sure, they do not represent the entire black community. By the same token, however, their injection of racial poison into the American bloodstream should not be permitted to go unchallenged. To date there has been an ominous silence on this score.

In a recent letter to the *New York Times*, Dr. Robert Gordis deplored this failure to speak out against black anti-Semitism:

As the group tensions become exacerbated, the silence of the Christian churches of New York and the nation, of individual ministers, priests, and laymen, as well as of organized Christian bodies, is deafening. This almost complete lack of response by the spokesmen for the Judeo-Christian moral tradition, in which I fervently believe, is particularly tragic in this year of grace.

It comes two decades after the tragic failure of the Christian church – except for a small group of great-souled Christian heroes and martyrs – to lift its voice against the horrors of the Nazi holocaust. Thus Christian leaders in the post-Nazi era continue to make the egregious blunder of regarding anti-Semitism as a Jewish issue and not as a Christian and human problem of massive dimensions. Their silence justifies the cynical observation that the only thing we learn from history is that we learn nothing from history.

There is a message in this theme for the American Jew as well. It is easy enough to point an accusing finger at others. It is tempting to salve our own consciences by calling attention to the moral failures in other people. But we have to make sure that we ourselves are not guilty of the very same sin of silence.

Are we using our voices sufficiently to further the rights of black Americans – yes, even in the face of perceptible anti-Semitism among a small minority of blacks? Are we permitting the reprehensible actions of a few to mute our voices of protest over the failure to implement the promise of American equality to our black fellow citizens?

Are we raising our voices sufficiently to convey to our public officials and to the newspapers our sentiments regarding the events in the Middle East, Jews in Arab countries, Jews behind the Iron Curtain?

As we face the festival of Purim, we would do well to remember the stern warning of Mordecai to Esther when he asked her to intercede with the King on behalf of her people. "For if you keep silent at a time like this…you and your father's house shall be destroyed."

Esther did not keep silent. Her speech saved her people at a time of great crisis. Let us make sure to speak out whenever our voices need to be heard. There may be more than gold in our speech. Life itself may depend on it.

1982/5742

Rabbi Sidney Greenberg

JEWISH IDENTITY

Taking Our Judaism Seriously

Time does not permit a rehearsal of the unbelievable ways Judaism has struck roots in American soil. I recommend to you Charles Silberman's excellent upbeat sociological study, "A Certain People." In it, he demonstrates to my satisfaction the enormous progress Jews and Judaism have made in America in recent decades.

But let me give one slight illustration to document his thesis.

About ten days ago, a sportswriter for the *New York Times* with the non-Jewish-sounding name, "George Vecsey," wrote a long piece passionately denouncing baseball, the management of the Mets and the Houston Astros, and the television industry for scheduling two Mets playoff games on Kol Nidre and Yom Kippur. He condemned this scheduling as an affront to the many loyal Jewish Mets fans and Jewish baseball fans in general. (Just for that, he predicted heavy rains would wash out the two games.) What his article said to me was, isn't it wonderful that even though there is no Jewish player on either team, there should be such sensitivity to Jewish values and sanctities as to elicit such a strong and vocal protest?

This is not to say that all is well with Judaism in America, that the Messiah has arrived. On the contrary, I am often pained by the sight of so many intelligent, well-educated Jewish men and women who are – Jewishly speaking – illiterate, who are totally innocent of any Jewish knowledge, loyalty, or commitment. They have, in fact, by their actions, passed the verdict on their vast Jewish heritage: "There's nothing there."

As I think of these people on this Yom Kippur, my heart weeps silently over the spiritual tragedy of so many of our people. Of course, a Jew has a right to reject his Judaism – but doesn't that very right impose a prior obligation to understand what it is he is rejecting?

As Jews, we pride ourselves on the freedom of thought we allow within our ranks – a latitude few other religions permit. But do we have a right to confuse freedom of thought with freedom *from* thought?

I have no quarrel with the Jew who studies Judaism, informs himself of its beliefs and doctrines, and then says, "I am sorry, I cannot accept that!" I may regret his conclusions, but I cannot challenge his right to them. They were arrived at honestly.

But does a Jew have the right to dismiss cavalierly, to reject out of hand, vast resources of mind and spirit which numberless Jews developed and preserved with their very lives? Does this not represent the most wanton kind of wastefulness? Does the right to be different give us the right to be indifferent?

As these thoughts lie heavy on my heart, there comes to mind the image of Franz Rosenzweig. Let me tell you about him.

The year is 1913. The place is a small Orthodox synagogue in a little German city called Cassel. The Yom Kippur services are in progress. The Cantor has already proclaimed the traditional formula before Kol Nidre: "With Divine sanction, and with the sanction of this holy congregation, we declare it lawful to pray together with those who have transgressed." Little does anyone suspect, however, that the congregation today includes a young man of 27 on the verge of the ultimate transgression. He has come to take last leave of Judaism before he embraces Christianity.

Franz Rosenzweig's brilliant mind had been nurtured on a heavy diet of philosophy. Of his own faith he knew pathetically little. Small wonder that it had offered him such meager sustenance. The teacher whom he revered most deeply was a Christian. One day Rosenzweig confronted him with a question freighted with a sense of personal urgency. "What would you do," he asked him, "if all answers fail?" The professor answered with soft earnestness: "I would go to the nearest church, kneel, and try to pray."

The impact of this answer upon the groping soul of the young man was profound. It crystallized into a fateful decision. He, too, would seek that same haven of secure refuge in the reassuring bosom of the church. Indeed, many Jews had already done so, frequently out of less pure motives. Many, like Heinrich Heine, had regarded the baptismal certificate as the ticket of admission to European society. Rosenzweig's integrity would not permit so sordid a spiritual transaction. He would turn to Christianity for the same rich rations which fed the inner hunger of his admired teacher.

But his systematic German mind laid down one condition. To become a Christian, he must arrive by way of Judaism. Was that not the path followed by the founders of Christianity? Rosenzweig would enter the door of the church not as a pagan but through the exit of the synagogue. And in what place and time could the official leave-taking of his people and his faith be effected more fittingly than in the synagogue on the Day of Atonement?

This was the mood in which Franz Rosenzweig entered the humble synagogue in Cassel on Yom Kippur 1913.

We know what he heard in the synagogue that Yom Kippur day. He heard what you and I shall hear during this sacred day:

He heard of a God who is near to all who call upon Him, to all who call upon Him in truth; a God who can be approached in honest confession by the humblest Jew without any human intermediary.

He heard of the eternal compassion of God for the folly and weakness of man.

He heard, in the *Haftorah* from Isaiah, the cry of God's messenger to undo the bands of the yoke, to let the oppressed go free, to deal bread to the hungry, to clothe the naked, to house the homeless.

He heard, in the story of the Jewish martyrs slaughtered for *Kiddush Hashem* by imperial Rome, the agonized cries of the anonymous Jewish spiritual heroes of all ages who were victimized but not vanquished.

He heard, in the story of Jonah, God's profound concern for the non-Jewish city of Nineveh, even for its beasts and cattle.

And when the shadows had fallen across the faces of the worshippers and the Shofar blast announced the end of the solemn day of fasting, Rosenzweig was still part of the congregation which rose to its feet and with one voice proclaimed the battle slogan of the Jew:

"*Sh'ma Yisrael Adonai Elohenu Adonai echad.*"

Soon thereafter it became apparent that that Yom Kippur day was indeed a day of conversion for Franz Rosenzweig. He converted to Judaism. What started out as a day of mean desertion was to become a day of momentous discovery.

Shortly thereafter he wrote to a friend, telling him that he had reversed his decision to become a Christian. "It no longer seems necessary to me and…no longer possible." In another letter he recognized the meaning of the church to the world – namely, that no one can reach the Father except through the Christian redeemer. But, he said, "The situation is quite different for one who does not have to reach the Father because he is already with Him."

World War I found Rosenzweig in a German uniform. From the Macedonian trenches, he would send postcards and letters to his mother daily and in them he would include some of the thoughts that were spilling over in him about his newly discovered faith.

In true motherly fashion, his mother treasured these cards and letters, and when he shed the uniform, he was to use these notes for his great work, *The Star of Redemption*, in which he sought to convey the vast richness of Judaism to a wavering generation. He organized and conducted an academy for Jewish learning in Frankfurt and thus exerted a personal, lasting influence upon hundreds of disciples who carried his name and his influence to Israel and America.

In 1922 Rosenzweig was stricken by a crippling paralysis which was accompanied by almost incessant pain. His limbs soon were reduced to uselessness. His nerves betrayed their function. After a few years, he could not move his head nor utter a sound. But he relentlessly pursued his translation of the Bible and his commentaries upon the Jewish prayers and liturgy. When he was powerless to write, he would indicate letters one by one on an alphabet chart to form words. When death finally released him at 42, it put to sleep a still vital, creative mind of a devout Jew.

I have told the story of Franz Rosenzweig at some length not for the benefit of those who are not here. To all of us here, Franz Rosenzweig speaks to a real challenge. For if those outside the synagogue have rejected Judaism too casually, we have accepted it too casually. There is not enough of a difference between them and ourselves. We have not made the effort to acquaint ourselves with Jewish history, its vocabulary, its literature, its teachings. We have grown too complacent to permit our ignorance of our heritage to disturb us. We have failed, also, to regard Judaism as a way of life which demands personal commitment in action not only on state occasions but every day of our lives.

Kol Nidre summons each of us to take our Judaism seriously. If we are casual Jews, there is a real danger that our children will be Jewish casualties. But if we individually strive to enrich our lives with the riches our ancestors have preserved for us, we will be giving living testimony that there is indeed in our heritage something great and beautiful there.

1986/5746

The Idols We Worship

Two seasoned sailors heard the chaplain preach on the Ten Commandments. When the sermon was over, one sailor muttered to his friend: "Well, at least I never made any graven images."

That sailor, like most of us, looked upon the worship of idols as an ancient practice, characteristic of primitive people. In fact, the second commandment has been called "the obsolete commandment." But is it? Has idolatry really disappeared in the twentieth century? Not if some of our most perceptive observers are to be believed. "Contemporary life," wrote philosopher Will Herberg, "is idolatry-ridden to an appalling degree."

In many of the cults that have proliferated in our time, idolatry has appeared in the blind, submissive worship of the guru, the infallible leader, the one who, through brainwashing, has gained even the power to command the believer to commit suicide at his behest. The tragedy of Jim Jones and the People's Temple in Guyana was the result of this insidious form of idolatry.

In his important book, *Crazy for God*, Christopher Edwards, a former Moonie, provides a glimpse into the nightmare of cult life and, in the process, reveals its idolatrous character. He shows us the Moonies swaying back and forth around a picture of the Reverend Moon, bowing down on command before the portrait, and praying to him as "Our new Messiah, the Creator and giver of true life…Father, we pledge our lives to you, our hearts, our souls!"

We human beings are born believers. Believing is as natural to us as breathing. When God departs, the little gods come rushing in, and some dark spirit will sit in his seat.

The brutal madness called Nazism dethroned God and replaced Him with a malicious idol. This grace was recited by small children in Nazi Germany: "Führer, my Führer, sent to me from God, protect and maintain me throughout my life. Thou who hast saved Germany from deepest need. I thank thee for my daily bread. Remain at my side and never leave me, Führer, my Führer, my faith, my light. Heil, my Führer."

The word "worship" is derived from an Old English word meaning "worth." That which assumes supreme worth in our eyes;

97

that is what we worship; that becomes our God. Understood in this light, it is not only cultists and Nazis who are idolaters.

We can and do make graven images of power, status, or wealth. On their altars, we bring supreme sacrifices. To obtain them, we often surrender our honor, compromise our character, neglect our families, and destroy our health.

A recent cartoon shows two aristocratic-looking gentlemen sitting in heavily upholstered chairs. One says to the other: "It was terrible! I dreamed the dollar was no longer worth worshipping!"

It is only when we understand the powerful appeal of idolatry that we appreciate why a Jew is expected to repeat morning and evening, every day of his life: "Hear O Israel, the Lord our God, the Lord is One."

God alone is to be worshipped. To Him alone we are to dedicate all that we are and all that we possess.

A shoe manufacturer condensed this whole philosophy of life in a small sign that sat on his desk: "God first, shoes second."

1979/5739

Book and Ladder

In 1990 the Council of Jewish Federations released the results of a National Jewish population study that set off bells of alarm and apprehension in the American Jewish community.

The most distressing statistic showed that between 1985 and 1990, 52% of the Jews in America who married, married non-Jews.

This compares with a 7% figure of intermarriage for those who married between 1940 and 1960, and that compares with a 3% intermarriage rate between 1900 and 1940.

Moreover, in families where there was only one Jewish parent, only 28% of the children were raised as Jews, 41% were raised in other faiths.

There was another cause for alarm. In 1960, two-thirds of Jewish children between the ages of 7 and 17 received a Jewish education. Today, that number has shrunk to 40%.

These chilling statistics gave rise to justifiable fears for our future as a distinct community, and gave shape to a new emphasis on the need for continuity. "Continuity" has surfaced as a very prominent word on the agenda of the American Jewish community. Jewish Federations in all our major cities have begun to reexamine their priorities in the allocation of communal funds.

Perhaps we were too shortsighted by focusing so heavily on the needs of Jews in Israel, Russia, Ethiopia. Perhaps too much of our communal energy was directed to doing for others. We must begin to focus more energy on our local needs.

Dr. Ismar Schorsch, Chancellor of the Jewish Theological Seminary, recently declared: "This is where the battlefield for Judaism is, not the Middle East. The enormous funds that American Jews sent to Israel for its welfare need to be shifted to Jewish education. The most pressing problem for the survival of world Jewry is the survival of American Jewry."

Every domestic Jewish institution must be strengthened in its capacity to be a more effective instrument for Jewish education, Jewish living, Jewish growing– for Jewish continuity. Not is it only in America that this message is being heard. Israel's Deputy Foreign Minister, Yossi Beilin, addressing an American Jewish audience, appeals to us to channel vast resources into Jewish education, Jewish summer camps, and youth pilgrimages to Israel. And out of Israel comes a report that the Foreign Ministry is currently examining a plan to bring 100,000 Jewish teenagers to Israel. The cost of the project is estimated at $250 million.

Instead of American Jews allocating funds to insure Israel's survival, Israel is now contemplating spending huge amounts of money from its meager resources to insure the survival of the American Jewish community – to insure our continuity.

The concern for Jewish continuity is shared by every Jew, no matter how minimal are his Jewish loyalties and commitments.

If a Jew still retains the tiniest spark of Jewish feeling, a *Yiddishe nishamah*, the prospect of the "Vanishing Jew" must generate genuine anxiety.

A telling witness of this truth is Leslie Fiedler, one of the leading students of literature on the American scene. He is a distinguished critic, lecturer, and writer. Every important literary magazine has published his writings. His most celebrated analysis of American literature appeared in *Love and Death in the American Novel*.

Once upon a time, when he was younger, he believed that all ethnic and religious differences should disappear in a global world, in a unified society. The whole human family should be one with all distinctiveness and differences bleached out.

But now he is in his late seventies and he has written a new collection of essays in a book called, *Fiedler on the Roof: Essays on Literature and Jewish Identity*. He describes the tragedy of his life. The last essay in the book is called, "In Every Generation," a play on words of the *Hagaddah*.

He who believed in one world now finds that his children and grandchildren have drifted away from Judaism. Listen to his lament: "In any case, there is no one to say *Kaddish* for me when I die. I am not just a minimal Jew, my Judaism, nearly non-existent, but as I have only recently become aware, a terminal one as well. The last of a 4,000 year line."

It is what he had in fact wanted. "From childhood on I dreamed a world without ethnic or religious divisions though I knew that this meant a world without Jews." He called this experience the "silent Holocaust." That is an end to a separate Jewish identity whether defined racially, religiously, or culturally. Now Fiedler writes, "I have discovered at long last that I am a Hebrew of Hebrews, Pharisee of Pharisees. Nothing to return to – nothing to hope for."

Marginal Jew though he is, he is profoundly pained for having worked and hoped for a rupture in Jewish continuity – for a world without Jews.

Let us now turn the spotlight from our Federations and from our "terminal" Jew and from Israel and focus it directly upon each of us.

What part does each of us personally play in addressing the challenge of Jewish continuity? No national Jewish organization or Federation or Israeli effort can do for us what only we ourselves can and must do to guarantee Jewish continuity. What we each can and must do is indicated in the number of the New Year we have so recently ushered in.

In Hebrew the letters by which we designate 5755 are *tuf, shin, nun* and *hey*. Those four letters can be read as, "*Tishneh*," which means, "You shall study."

When we utter the phrase "Jewish education" we think reflexively of children, religious schools, day schools, *yeshivot*, Camp Ramah. But Jewish study is not exclusively a children's occupation. Judaism is not a kiddy shop. In life's shopping center it is not located in the juvenile section. Judaism is a faith for all seasons – indeed, a lifelong quest. The study of our magnificent heritage is a continuous obligation and privilege contributing to our spiritual and intellectual growth.

"*Tishneh*" speaks to each and every one of us no matter how learned we already are, how deep our understanding of our accumulated religious treasures and texts.

One East European Jewish community dismissed its rabbi because the lights in his study were not burning past midnight.

"The failure for most American Jews is that Judaism is a closed book," said Steven Bayme, national director of Jewish Communal Affairs at the American Jewish Committee. "We always prided ourselves as being people of the book. Unfortunately today our capacity to read a Jewish book in the original language has been

101

sharply diminished. We insist on the highest standards in our secular education, but we have yet to transmit that to our Jewish education."

We in our community are so extravagantly blessed by so many opportunities for adult Jewish education. In addition to the classes offered by each congregation, we have Gratz College and the Reconstructionist Rabbinical College offering such a rich variety of Jewish educational experiences.

And if for very compelling reasons we cannot join a class to further our Jewish knowledge we can read Jewish books so readily available to all of us. Is it too much to ask of ourselves that we read at least one Jewish book a month?

Jewish continuity is intimately related to Jewish content, and Jewish content is acquired through study.

The same four Hebrew letters which spell out the number of the New Year on the calendar can be vocalized to read, "*Tishaneh*," which means, "You shall change."

For all people, fall marks the change of seasons. For Jews, fall marks the season of changes. This, in fact, is precisely the meaning of our High Holy Days. They are designed to stimulate us to make the necessary changes in our personal lives and in our Jewish lives, if indeed they can be separated. The High Holy Days say to each of us not only that we *should* change but also that we *can* change.

This is not a popular truth. We all have heard, and probably uttered, the tired adage, "You can't teach an old dog new tricks. You can't change human nature." Maybe. But it is human nature to change human action. If we couldn't change, our High Holy Days would be a cruel hoax, summoning us to do what can't be done. But Judaism most empathically assures us that what *should* be done *can* be done. We can grow morally, emotionally, and spiritually. We are not prisoners of our past.

Judaism says to us, "It only takes one person to change your life; that person is you." And if we are truly concerned about Jewish continuity, there are *changes* in our Jewish behavior that we each can and should make.

Professor Abraham Heschel who himself was a totally observant Jew once gave us this wonderful prescription for a healthier Jewish community. He said that we have to lower a ladder in the valley and say to every Jew: "Climb as high as you can and then a little higher than you can."

He wasn't asking any Jew to become a totally observant Jew, although I'm sure he would not feel terribly hurt if anyone did. What he urged was: do as much as you can. Climb one rung of the ladder at a time. When you are ready, climb one rung higher. Start somewhere with one step. Light Shabbat candles. Make Friday night family night. Make the blessing over the wine. Make a *motzi* over the bread. Make a *motzi* at the dinner meal every night. Eliminate *treif* food from the home. Eliminate it from your diet outside the home. Call a lonely person. Stop gossiping. Give *tzedakah* regularly.

If we each want to add a link to the Jewish generations, if we are genuinely concerned about Jewish continuity, if we want Judaism to prosper in America as the Jew has prospered, if we want future generations of American Jews to find in their identity, joy, meaning, and inspiration, let us listen to the call letters of 5755:

> *Tishneh* – You shall study! Open the book!
> *Tishaneh* – You shall change! Climb the ladder!

And as we do so we will faithfully discharge the responsibilities that are uniquely ours. For only we can provide Jewish homes for our children in which Judaism is experienced in joy as something beautiful and meaningful. Only we can endow them with memories that will link them to our past and make them dedicated to our future.

You and I are the central actors in the unfolding drama of Jewish continuity. Each of us has a vital role to play. And we must play it as effectively as we can so that the glorious 4,000-year-old odyssey of our people might continue into the uncharted future, and thus continue to enrich the lives of its adherents as well as the larger human family.

1995/5755

A Work of Heaven

A lady trying to impress her neighbors at a banquet table steered the conversation around to the subject of genealogy. This gave her the opportunity to boast that she traced her ancestry back to one of the signers of the Declaration of Independence. Then turning to the lady to her right she asked,

"And how far back do your family records go, my dear?"

"I really can't say for sure," came the reply with a touch of vinegar. "You see, my dear, all our family records were destroyed by Noah's flood."

We Jews, in our collective memory, remember back to the days of Noah and even before, back to the very dawn of creation. Our history is measured in millennia. A single century on the Jewish calendar is not an impressive slice of time.

And yet it is altogether fitting that we should mark with genuine joy and fervent thanksgiving a full century of growth and achievement by The Jewish Theological Seminary of America, the mother institution of the Conservative Movement. Indeed it can be convincingly argued that the last 100 years have constituted the most eventful century in the entire sweep of Jewish history.

Two of the momentous events of our recent past come readily to mind – the inconsolable murder of the Six Million and the exhilarating rebirth of the State of Israel. Less dramatic but no less significant in our historical perspective has been the emergence of the American Jewish community – the largest Jewish community in the world today and indeed in all of Jewish history.

The Seminary has contributed most impressively to the emotional health of that community, its positive acceptance of its identity, the strength and texture of its spiritual fabric.

Great truths are often captured in symbols. I find it enormously suggestive that the biblical theme chosen to be engraved in stone over the entrance to the Seminary is the symbol of the burning bush, accompanied by the Torah's description of that revolutionary moment in Moses' life: "And the bush was not consumed."

The refusal of the bush to submit to the destructive flames that threatened to destroy it was symbolic of the faith of the Seminary's founders and spiritual architects that Judaism would survive and flourish in American soil. It would succumb neither to the fires of discrimination nor to the flames of assimilation.

This faith was not too widely shared. Many a devout nineteenth-century European Jew mourned the child who left for America, the *trefa medina* (non-Kosher state). America might prove hospitable to the Jew, but it would prove fatal to Judaism. Spiritually speaking, there was nothing there. In Abraham Cahan's epic novel, *The Rise of David Levinsky*, the hero tells us what happened when he told his Talmud *rebbe* in Eastern Europe that he was thinking of leaving for the United States. "To America!" the *rebbe* shouts. "Lord of the World! But one becomes a Gentile there."

Nor were these fears altogether without justification. Many an immigrant threw his *tallit* and *tefillin* into the Atlantic from the deck of the ship carrying him to America, and his first American haircut often claimed his beard and *payot,* too. Tragically, too many of those who remained behind were to be consumed by the flames of the Holocaust.

Those who founded the Seminary knew full well the dangers confronting Jewish survival in America. Indeed it was those very dangers that conferred added urgency to their efforts. But the burning bush, which refused to be consumed, was a dramatic reminder of the capacity of Judaism throughout its long and perilous history to survive every threat of its existence.

If Moses could hear the Divine voice speak from amidst the bush, assuring him that the ground on which he stood was holy ground, surely there was no reason to despair in America. If holy ground could be found in the bleak, uncharted desert, who had the right to give up hope on the hospitable soil of this new home? Judaism could indeed thrive and prosper here. This faith fueled their hope and elicited their most determined efforts.

At the burning bush, Moses also received a divine mandate. He was to go back to his people in Egypt with a message they desperately needed to hear. He was to speak to them in the name of the God of their ancestors, who was mindful of their present tribulations, and who would bring them redemption. Thus, Moses was to speak to the Israelites in terms of their past, their present, and their future. In a true sense, this has been the mandate of Conservative Judaism from its inception: highest fidelity to our collective past, profoundest concern with our contemporary situation, and unwavering commitment to our creative future.

Fidelity to our past is exemplified by the highest standards of scholarship by both the Seminary's faculty and students. Note some of the myriad of outstanding alumni of the Seminary: Mordecai M. Kaplan, Louis Finkelstein, Gerson Cohen, Robert Gordis, Milton Steinberg, Simon Greenberg, and Moshe Greenberg.

Concern with our future is reflected in our unrivaled network of Ramah camps in America and Israel, in Neve Schechter, the Melton Research Center, and Prozdor, the Seminary's high school department.

At the bush, Moses was also given a message to deliver to the Pharaoh. Here perhaps, we can find one of the crucial dimensions that was to characterize Conservative Judaism. It was to be able to speak not only to the Jewish community, but also to the American non-Jewish community. It had to believe and act on the belief that the message of Judaism needed to be heard and understood by all of America. This conviction that Judaism could not only survive in America but could actually enrich America with its distinctive genius and unique message was responsible for the creation of a host of powerful instruments:

> the nationally broadcast, award-winning Eternal Light programs on radio and television which interpret the Jewish tradition to mass audiences;

> the Institute for Religious and Social Studies which brings together clergymen of all faiths;

> the Conference on Science, Religion, and Philosophy which explores moral issues of common concern to all theologians;

> its unrivaled library which is used by scholars of all religions;

its magnificent Jewish Museum, which is visited annually by thousands of people of all faiths who see the impressive evidence of Jewish artistic creativity;

training scores of Rabbis and Scholars who teach Judaism on college campuses throughout America and in Israel; and

holiday messages published in the leading American newspapers. These messages draw upon the Jewish heritage to shed light on the spiritual concerns of America.

Emerson once wrote, "An institution is the lengthened shadow of a man." The man who left the largest and most enduring impact on the character of the Seminary was Solomon Schechter. The words he spoke in 1913, at the founding meeting of The United Synagogue, are as true today as when he uttered them:

It is real work of heaven for which I invite your attention and participation – a work on which, in my humble opinion, depends the continuance and the survival of traditional Judaism in this century.

If we turn Emerson's statement around, it yields another important truth. A man is the lengthened shadow of an institution. We rabbis are most assuredly reflective of the blessed influence of the Seminary upon our lives. There we found our holy ground. There we heard the redemptive and inspiring message to speak to our fellow Jews and to the non-Jewish world. There we were proudly summoned to participate and to invite others to participate with us in "a real work of heaven."

1988/5748

107

We All Lean

Every morning, with unfailing regularity, the local telephone company would get a call from the same person asking for the exact time. This went on for several weeks. Finally, the telephone operator could not restrain her curiosity about the identity of the caller. So, one day, when the expected call arrived, she said to the caller,

"I can't help wondering who you are and why you call every day."

"I work at the Reliable Steel Company," she answered, "and we need to know the precise moment to blow the noon whistle."

Hearing this, the telephone operator burst into laughter. "That's funny," she said, "we set our time by the noon whistle."

I am writing this on the day after the conclusion of *Pesach* with some of its magnificent themes still lingering on. The anecdote illustrates one of the supreme truths underlined by one of the Four Questions. "On this night we all lean." But it is not only at the Seder that we all lean. We always lean heavily on one another. Like the whistle blower and the telephone operator, we need each other if we are to perform our tasks effectively.

Consider how many people we lean on just to get through each day of our lives. We get up in the morning and our homes are warm because there are people making sure that a supply of electricity or gas is reaching us. We want to know the weather forecast so we'll know how to dress. We flick on the radio and it works, again because the electricity is there and the whole crew at the radio station is functioning properly. We get the temperature reading because the countless people at the weather bureau have gathered the data and interpreted it for us. And our telephone is working, and there is food available for breakfast thanks to the continued efforts of literally hundreds of people. No fewer than 240 people are involved between the time that wheat is planted and a loaf of bread appears on our table. We're leaning on so many people and we have barely started our day.

And how about the benefactors long gone upon whom we lean for so much? The faith that sustains us, the books that instruct us, the medicines that heal us, the music that inspires us, the art that uplifts us, the inventions that serve us – if we were to draw up an inventory in the spirit of *Dayenu*, where would it end?

This journal marks the celebration of Temple Sinai's eighteen years in Dresher, Pennsylvania. To reach this coveted milestone, it leaned heavily on the loyalty, faithfulness, and sacrifice of countless people, living and dead. Even this celebratory journal owes its success to the many, many people on whom it leaned for support and sustenance.

We can say with justifiable pride that, for more than a half century, several generations have leaned on Temple Sinai to provide them with a knowledge of their heritage, a respect for their past, a hope for their future.

The kind of future Judaism will enjoy in our community, and in our country, depends intimately on the personal efforts of each of us, on the depth of our commitment, the constancy of our loyalty, the faithfulness of our observance. Future generations are leaning on us. Let's be good to them.

1978/5738

Faith in Ourselves

Professor Charles Eliot, who was president of Harvard University from 1869 to 1909, once had occasion to dedicate a new hall of philosophy and he was searching for an appropriate inscription to place above its entrance.

After much deliberation with his faculty members, he announced his choice – the maxim of Protagoras: "Man is the measure of all things." With that decision made, the faculty adjourned for the summer vacation.

When school reopened in the fall, the faculty was surprised to find that Eliot had apparently had a change of heart. Instead of the inscription they had discussed, he had used the words of the psalmist: "What is man that Thou art mindful of him?" (*Psalms* 8:5)

Eliot was obviously ambivalent in his estimate of man's significance. Nor was he alone in that regard. We hear echoes of Eliot's indecisiveness in the rabbinical comments on the order of creation as described in this week's Torah portion. Why, asked the ancient sages, was man created last?

One sage attributed the reason to man's supreme significance:

Just as a mortal king, when he invites someone very dear to him, prepares an elaborate meal and comfortable sleeping quarters for his guest, and only then does he summon his guest, so too, God first prepared food and shelter. That is, He created the grass, vegetables, trees and animals, and only on the sixth day, when all was in readiness, did He invite His beloved guest, man, to come and partake of this glory.

A second sage disagreed. Man's late creation, he believed, is a sign of his insignificance. "Man was the last to be created so that, should he become proud and inflated, he may be reminded that the lowly flea preceded him in the order of creation."

In spite of such occasional expressions of doubt in man's value and ultimate significance, there can be no question that one of the basic principles of our faith is the belief that man was created "in the image of God." Yes, man's origin is the lowly earth. But at creation, God breathed His Divine spirit into him, and that spirit became his patent of nobility. In fact, even the psalmist who asked, "What is man that Thou art mindful of him?" went on almost immediately to answer his own question: "Nevertheless, Thou hast made him but a little less than divine."

This faith in man was never easy to embrace, and living as we do in a post-Holocaust world, it is more difficult than ever before. And yet without this faith, where can we find hope for progress and human betterment? Unless we believe in man's potential goodness and inherent sanctity, we have neither reason to believe in his ability to govern himself wisely nor to respect his rights.

Democracy has this faith in man. It declares: "We hold these Truths to be self-evident, that all men are created equal, that they are endowed by their Creator with certain inalienable Rights, that among these are Life, Liberty and the Pursuit of Happiness."

Notice, democracy does not try to prove man's rights. It calls them "self-evident" truths, a non-theological equivalent for faith. Because democracy has this faith in man, it permits him to determine for himself who shall rule him and how, what if anything he will believe, what and when he shall speak.

Dictatorships, whether of the left or right, reject this faith in man. Otto Strasser, in *Hitler and I*, quotes the malevolent demon of Nazism as saying, "From this conviction I will never depart. ...Man is congenitally evil. He can only be controlled by force. To govern him, everything is permissible. You must lie, betray, even kill when policy demands it."

Notice again, Hitler did not attempt to prove why he lacked faith in man. He called it a "conviction." His lack of faith in man was also a matter of faith. And because dictators reject any faith in man, they determine who will rule him and how, what and when he will speak. They ultimately also determine how and whether he shall live.

In the final analysis, therefore, whether we believe in man or not determines his very fate.

And our own fate also hinges on this question. Unless we believe in the good in ourselves, we shall never realize it. The surest way of becoming moral failures is to convince ourselves that we can never overcome our moral shortcomings.

The only way to bring out the best in ourselves is to believe that it is there and that the Almighty did indeed fashion us, only a little less than divine.

When we are about to despair in man, it is helpful to realize how far he has developed and in how short a time. To get a vivid picture of human achievement in its proper perspective, let us compress all of human history into twelve hours – the time it takes the small hand on our watches to make one complete revolution.

Well, if we did that, it would take until a quarter to 12 before man abandoned his habits as a wandering hunter and become domesticated. At 7 minutes to 12, he would learn how to write. At 3 minutes to 12, he would learn the Ten Commandments. And at a few seconds before 12, he would be sitting in Independence Hall drawing up the Declaration of Independence.

When we look at man in this light, we see that spiritually he is still in his infancy. He is now only beginning to walk, and how depressed we are when we see him fail, thinking in our impatience that he will never be able to walk at all.

Perhaps in terms of what still remains to be done, man still has a long way to go. But in terms of what he has already accomplished, he has come a long, long way.

Disraeli once wrote, "The greatest thing you can do for another is not just to share your riches, but to reveal to him his own."

That's what the Torah did for each of us. It reminded us of our vast spiritual inheritance, for after all, did God not fashion us in His image?

1995/5755

At the Bar of Judgment

The secular New Year, which begins on January 1, is ushered in by most Americans in a spirit of reckless self-abandon. Every device, both artificial and expensive, is adopted to help one forget oneself, to help one escape from oneself. And the extent of the success of the New Year's celebration is very often determined by the number of its participants who have lately lost self-consciousness, or at the very least, self-control. In bold and startling contrast to this method of ushering in a New Year, there is the Jewish conception which has for its goal not self-forgetfulness but self-awareness, not escape from ourselves but rather a deliberate concentration upon ourselves, not self-abandon but self-control. *Rosh Hashanah* is the day of moral inventory, when we focus the spotlight of conscience upon ourselves and declare with Pope: "The proper study of mankind is man." And in this process of taking stock of ourselves, the dominant motif is one of judgment. As a matter of fact, *Rosh Hashanah* is referred to throughout the liturgy as the *"Yom HaDin"* – The Day of Judgment. And the active Jewish genius has even supplied the picturesque details of the procedure in the Heavenly Court as the soul of man appears before the Divine Judge: "The great trumpet is sounded; the still small voice is heard; the angels are dismayed; fear and trembling seize hold of them as they proclaim, 'Behold the Day of Judgment.'"

If then we are to conform to the spirit of the day, we should use this day as an occasion for self-judgment, self-examination, and self-criticism. But by what standards shall we judge ourselves? With which questions shall we cross-examine ourselves? In every search for truth, the important thing is to be able to ask the right question. The skillful attorney is the one who can, by a well-pointed question, elicit the information he desires. So too, as we prepare to take ourselves to task, we must be able to frame the significant questions. What are those questions?

On this point too, Jewish tradition has something to say. In the Talmud, our sages reveal to us basic questions that are put to the individual, at the Heavenly bar of justice. And while our sages project these questions into the hereafter, I think it is well that we put these questions to ourselves in the here and now. The student who knows the question that will appear on the examination paper is at an obvious advantage. He knows exactly how to prepare and upon which subjects to concentrate. Perhaps we too shall be better equipped to answer the soul-examining questions at the Heavenly bar of judgment if we learn them now, and attempt to evaluate our accomplishments in terms of these measuring rods.

Rava said, "At the hour when one is brought to judgment, he is asked, 'Have you dealt with honesty? Did you set aside appointed hours for the study of Torah? Did you understand the implication of things? Did you hope for salvation?'" It is upon these soul-searching questions that we are going to dwell this morning. Let us consider them more carefully.

The first question we shall have to answer concerns our personal integrity. "Did you deal with honesty? Did you carry your high-sounding ideals into the marketplace, did you apply them in actual life, did you allow them to guide your actions, or did you permit them to remain empty phrases without any meaning in your daily behavior?" This is indeed a basic question, for unless we can answer in the affirmative, we can never hope to build a society that shall be honest. Plato, long ago, truly pointed out that the state is the individual writ large. The state is a magnified version of the people who compose it, and it is impossible to have a just society unless the people who compose that society are just. And further, how can we hope and work for universal justice, for universal honesty, unless we are so convinced of their worth that we first live by them in our own personal lives? Certainly, we can have little reason to fight for justice if we will not respect it in our dealings with our fellow man. If honesty disappears as a personal ideal, it can have no meaning as a universal ideal. We cannot die for justice if we will not live by it.

And there is yet perhaps a deeper reason why the question of personal integrity is so basic today. Our generation has witnessed the painful spectacle of the collapse of all the ideals and values in which we were taught to believe and in terms of which we had hoped to build our dreams of a brighter tomorrow. Only yesterday, our schools and teachers were promising us that science would create the tools to reduce the drudgery of work and enable man to enjoy life, that democracy would extend its sway throughout the world, that international good-will would displace war, that group prejudices and hatreds would melt before the sun of universal enlightenment. We had the faith that a more ideal world was within our reach – a world of universal abundance of freedom and peace.

Today these dreams are scattered. There is little faith left in us. And what we badly need is something we can hold onto, something we can believe in. Where then are we to find that staying power if not within ourselves? Today, personal integrity is an absolute necessity. If our inner selves betray us, we shall not find faith living anywhere else. Have you dealt with honesty?

Question number two: "Did you set aside appointed hours for the study of Torah?" This question assumes special relevance and importance today. Never was there so little knowledge about Judaism and never was it so badly needed. We have many Jews who possess a high degree of general culture but who are Jewishly illiterate. And very often this ignorance of Judaism is accompanied by a sense of complacency, if not pride. It is by no means rare to meet Jews who regard their total unfamiliarity with Judaism as a sign of modernity.

Out of this soil of ignorance there have sprouted the psychic disorders of so many modern Jews – their lack of spiritual roots, their sense of homelessness, their failure to achieve dignity and poise, their defenselessness in the hour of peril. So many of our people have developed an inferiority complex. They have actually begun to believe the malicious propaganda spread by our enemies. The very fact that we are persecuted is sufficient proof for them that we deserve it. "Where there's smoke, there's fire," they mutter in shame.

A particularly painful example of this self-hatred appeared a few months ago when a fellow Jew, Milton Mayer, writing in the *Saturday Evening Post,* accused the Jews of every vice; and many other Jews echoed his words and added a great, "Amen." They blamed upon themselves or, as was more frequently the case, upon each other, every sin he mentioned. And yet Wendel Wilkie, writing in a subsequent issue of the same magazine, said, "I can find only disease and death in the wailing distortion of Mr. Milton Mayer's recent flagellation of the Jews."

Only the knowledge of our tradition can spare us the sense of shame that ignorance brings. Only if we study our heritage can we be insulated against the shocks of a hostile world. If we know what

Judaism stands for, we would understand why Nazism is trying so fearfully and desperately to eradicate it. We would understand why Hitler feels that God must go if he is to remain. Knowing this would bring us a sense of pride. We might even feel that to be singled out by the Nazis as their worst enemy is for us a great distinction. A man is not only known by the friends he keeps. A man may also be known by the enemies he makes. Did you set aside appointed hours for the study of Torah?

Question number three: "Did you understand the implication of things?" Or if applied to the modern scene, "Do you understand the implication of the present world crisis?" Crisis may sometimes prove rewarding because it points to the presence of an evil and helps to eradicate it, just as a fever is in a sense beneficial since it reveals the presence of a germ. But a crisis will only have meaning when we can see beneath the surface and discern the causes deeper down – the factors that elude the eyes and yet are the real forces in the catastrophe. If we understand our contemporary crisis correctly, we will find that it is due to the spiritual bankruptcy of our age – the failure of our spiritual progress to keep pace with our mechanical progress.

According to an old story, a Greek painter created what he thought was his masterpiece – a picture of a farmer holding a cluster of grapes. Whoever saw it marveled at its naturalness. But the artist himself was not convinced. So, in order to test the genuineness of his painting, he placed it among some shrubbery in a thick forest. Soon birds flocked to the painting and began to peck at the painted grapes. The artist's friends applauded loudly. Nothing they said could better prove the skill of the artist than the fact that the painting had so completely deceived the birds. The artist, however, lashed the picture and tore it to shreds. "If the painting had been true," he cried, "the birds would have refrained from pecking at the grapes for they would have been afraid of the farmer holding the grapes. The grapes are satisfactory, but the man is a failure."

Yes, my friends, the grapes are satisfactory, but the man is a failure. The tools that man holds in his hands are satisfactory, but he himself is a failure. We have learned how to conquer disease and postpone death, but we have not learned how to live life. We may be experts in sanitation but not in sanity. We have built bridges and tunnels, but neither above nor below the earth have we found true happiness. We have perfected the speed of communication but we have not quickened the soul. We have learned how to gain a good livelihood but we have not achieved a rich life. We've learned to fly in the air like birds, we've learned to swim the ocean like fish, but we've yet to learn to walk the earth like men. In our concern with things, with buildings and machines, we forgot the warning of the poet who said:

> We are blind until we see
> That is the human plan
> Nothing is worth the making
> If it does not make the man!
> Why build these cities glorious
> If man unbuilded goes
> In vain we build the world
> Unless the builder also grows.

Yes, we have forgotten to build the builder. We have forgotten to build the spirit of man. We thought that training the mind made training of character unnecessary. Why the religious school? Is not the public school sufficient? Why synagogues? Aren't there libraries? Do you understand the implication of the present world crisis?

Question number four: "Did you hope for salvation?" A few years ago we might have dismissed this question very lightly. We did not realize then perhaps how close despair is to defeat. But our sages long ago pointed out that, when hope goes, everything goes with it. They noticed that when Moses pleaded against being appointed leader over the Israelites in Egypt, he protested to God, "Behold, they will not believe me." He used the word "Behold" in Hebrew, "*Hen.*" And when God announced to Moses that his end had come, the Lord said, "Behold your days have drawn near to death." Again "Behold," "*Hen,*" was used. This similarity of expression led our sages to comment. "*B'shaah sheamarta hen lo yaaminu bee, hen karvu yamekha lamut.*" God says to Moses, "At the moment you said 'Behold, they will not believe Me,' at that moment your death began." When Moses lost hope, he lost life itself. Conversely, if we are to maintain life, we must desperately cling to hope.

117

Present-day events have more than justified the insight of our sages. Since the war broke out, news reporters and commentators have been stressing the reality and the power of forces other than tanks, guns, and planes. We've heard repeated emphasis falling upon words like "morale," "determination," "will," "hope." Of special interest are the words of the deposed President of Czechoslovakia, who certainly would have been justified in giving up hope, and yet he said:

> Man, as long as he is alive, must never give up optimistic idealism. He must never, even if he sees the real situation in rather dark colors, cease to hope for better times and he must, most of all, never cease to work for them, never cease to struggle for them and never be discouraged on his way by any ill success.

I am aware of the fact that many of us would desperately like to develop hope and yet are unable to do so. Where can we find a source of hope?

Towards the beginning of the past century, the British were hard-pressed by a powerful foe. One day, a young lieutenant rushed with a map into the tent of the English General Wellington and hysterically cried, "Look, General, Napoleon's Army is almost upon us!" "Get larger maps and the enemy won't seem so close," was the answer. If the present is critical, if the enemy seems to be almost upon us, let us get larger maps. Let us use larger segments of time to rest our perspective and courage. What we need is the ability to look at the fleeting and foreboding present against the background of a stable and reassuring past.

When the Roman legions had burned the Temple and were laying waste the cities and villages of Palestine, there were many who said, "Jewry is doomed, this is the end." But Jewry soon recovered. It was not the end.

When in 1348 the Black Plague was sweeping destructively through Europe claiming half the population as its victims, there were many who said, "Europe is perishing, this is the end." But Europe recovered; it was not the end.

When the Civil War was raging in our own country in 1864, there must have been many who said, "The Union is doomed, this is the end." But the Union survived. It was not the end.

The dictators may arrogantly strut across the map of the world, but they lord over it only for a day. They win the battle but they cannot, and will not, win the war. The lesson of history is clear. The forces of darkness retard but they do not permanently check their march of progress. Their empire is built on destruction and violence. It must end in destruction and violence. True, the wounds and hurts of countless numbers of innocent men and women, which the tyrants have inflicted, will long live on. A mother's heart does not heal easily. But humanity will recover. It is not the end. After the clouds and the storm will have passed, the sun will shine again and mankind – a mankind that will be purer for having been cleansed in fire and wiser for having been made aware of its mistakes – will press on with renewed strength. Have you hoped for salvation?

These then are the four questions that we must answer before the bar of Divine Justice. Let us therefore on this preparatory day of judgment, resolve to plot our course of action for the year that lies ahead in such a way that, on next *Rosh Hashanah*, when we cross-examine ourselves and ask, "Have I dealt with honesty to maintain my faith? Have I set aside appointed hours for the study of Torah, to spare myself a sense of shame and give me a sense of pride? Have I understood the implication of the present catastrophe, to realize the importance of the spiritual in life? Did I hope for salvation upon which victory depends?" To all these we will be able to answer and say, "Oh Lord, I have done Thy will."

1989/5749

Rabbi Sidney Greenberg

SOME CLOSING THOUGHTS

Completing Life

I wonder how many of us in the congregation recognize the name, Randy Shilts. But when he died at the age of 43, he left behind an impressive literary harvest. His monumental history of AIDS, *And the Band Played On*, was made into a movie and was nominated for all kinds of Emmy Awards.

Shilts was a journalist for the *San Francisco Chronicle*. He was the first full-time reporter on AIDS for a major American daily, and he did as much as anyone to publicize the epidemic. At his death, *Newsweek* noted his passing with a full-page article titled, "And the Band Stopped Playing." Death interrupted his writing as he raced to finish his third book, *Conduct Unbecoming – A History of Homosexuals in the American Military*.

When he was in the final stages of his disease, he was interviewed on television and he was asked how he felt knowing that his life was soon to end. Here is how he answered the question:

"You have the feeling that your life is finished but not completed."

Those are gripping words. I believe they touch each of us at the very core of our souls. At whatever age our lives will be finished, will we have the feeling that they are not completed?

Perhaps it is inevitable that no life is ever fully completed. Moses never enters the Promised Land. Schubert is not the only composer who leaves an unfinished symphony. Christopher Morley wrote that, "We are each a folder of unfinished business." But what can we do to complete as much of our lives as possible during our days on this earth?

Dr. Abraham Maslow, the noted psychologist, has estimated that the average human being achieves only seven percent of his potential.

Would anyone be content with such a slim percentage of success in any field of endeavor? I don't imagine any farmer would be too happy or win any ribbons at the county fair if his wheat fields or his apple orchards yielded only seven percent of their potential. Should we rest content with such a meager human harvest?

Among his literary remains, Nathaniel Hawthorne left some notebooks that contain random ideas he jotted down as they occurred to him. One of the short entries reads as follows:

"Suggestion for a story – story in which the principal character simply never appears."

Unhappily, this is the story of too many lives. The principal character simply never appears. The person we might grow into, the human being we might become, doesn't show up.

Our potential greatness lies unrealized, the splendor remains imprisoned, the promise unfulfilled. Our lives develop a static character.

We stop growing morally, spiritually, and intellectually. We do not expand our sympathies. We do not enlarge our interests. We do not further our knowledge. We do not strengthen our self-control. We remain essentially where we were last year, five years ago, twenty years ago.

Whatever our age, it is a time for us to grow – to become more capable of forgiveness, more sensitive to another's pain, more receptive to criticism, more open to a new idea. We must never forget the principal character that is waiting to appear, urging us to complete as much of our lives as possible before they are finished.

In addition to striving to grow, there is another crucial requirement if we are to move towards a more complete life: we must repair the relationships with loved ones and friends that have become frayed, strained, or fractured. We must try to eliminate the festering angers, the accumulated resentments, the hurtful memories, the "foibles" we have nurtured much too long. This emotional garbage only poisons our systems and casts a cloud over our days.

A young man whose father was about to undergo very serious surgery was asked by a close friend, "What would you do if you knew your father was going to die tomorrow?" The son thought for a long moment and then sped away to his father's hospital beside. In the hospital, the young man went up to his father, who had been an alcoholic, and said, "Dad, there were times you beat me, locked me in the trunk of the car, and did other things to me, but I want you to know I love you and forgive you." They embraced and cried. The father came through the surgery without difficulty.

We call this holy day *Yom Kippur* but, in the Torah and in our liturgy, the day is always called *Yom Kippurim* (plural "forgivenesses"). We ask God to forgive us. We must forgive too.

God has built into each of us a garbage disposal. Let's use it. We'll feel so much cleaner and better when we do. And perhaps even healthier.

Perhaps in addition to a catalogue of our sins, we should have another list for "I forgive":

I forgive my parents for not being perfect and all-knowing as I believed as a child.

I forgive friends with whom I was once close, who evolved in different directions, and I forgive the special people who told me they'd love me forever, who moved on to loving others.

I forgive teachers who told me I didn't have certain abilities, whom I believed, and I forgive all the people who helped shape the inner boundaries that have kept me back, that I've had to work so hard to break through.

I forgive people for their troubled pasts and I allow them to move on and grow, and I forgive myself for bouts of inappropriate judgments, meanness of spirit, pettiness, envy, greed, weakness, and unjust anger.

I forgive people for not being more like me.

I forgive God for not being able to make everything better.

I forgive myself for being human and I accept myself in my imperfect humanity.

My friend and colleague, Rabbi Harold Schulweiss, has something very wise to say about *completing life*. In addition to continued growth and learning to forgive, he shares with us something he learned in his hospital bed while recovering from a heart attack: the importance of recognizing the enormity of the gift of each day and using it as wisely and as fully as we can. "This moment, this hour, this day is most important. Do you know whether you will have another like this one? Do not neglect the present tense.

"In the hospital," he goes on, "I remembered what my mother told me when she was in the hospital. She always spoke to me in English, except this time. In Yiddish, she whispered, 'You know, if I get well I promise you I will know how to live better.' I don't know precisely what she had in mind, because she never had the chance. For her the rediscovery came too late." We need not wait for a calamitous event to open our eyes to this hour and to those who are about us.

The New Year begins when we each do our very best to complete our lives by striving mightily to keep growing, by repairing the relationships that need mending, and by making the most of each God-given day. In short, by inviting the principal character to appear, then we might each say in the words of Robert Frost: "The woods are lovely dark and deep and I have promises to keep and miles to go before I sleep." Let's keep the promise. Let's walk the miles all through 5755.

1995/5755

About the Author

Rabbi Sidney Greenberg was a world-renowned author, congregational rabbi, and lecturer until his death in 2003. In 1942, he was a founder of Temple Sinai in Philadelphia, where he led his congregation to its second location in Dresher, Pennsylvania until he retired in 1993. During his distinguished career, he taught Homiletics at the Reconstructionist Rabbinical College, the Jewish Theological Seminary, and Hebrew Union College. In 1992, he was honored by the Jewish Theological Seminary as "Rabbi of the Year." That same year, Temple Sinai named its sanctuary in his and his wife, Hilda's, honor. He authored more than 30 books, including *A Treasury of Comfort, Say Yes to Life*, and numerous prayer books used in congregations throughout the United States. He was also a featured columnist for the *Philadelphia Inquirer* and the *Jewish Exponent*.

Rabbi Greenberg was born and raised in New York City and received his undergraduate degree from Yeshiva University. He was ordained in 1942 by the Jewish Theological Seminary, which later awarded him the Doctor of Hebrew Letters degree. He served in the United States Air Force as Chaplain in World War II, for two years.

Printed in the United States
18557LVS00006B/205-315